—The Land of—
NARNIA

Brian Sibley Explores the World of C.S. Lewis

The Land of
NARNIA

Brian Sibley Explores the World of C.S. Lewis

with illustrations by Pauline Baynes

COLLINS LIONS

For
my God-daughters
CLAIRE, EMILY and MADELEINE,
my young friend
JAMIE MAGNUS STONE
and my grown-up friend
DAVE HEWSON
all of whom love
The Land of Narnia

First published in Great Britain in 1989
by Collins Lions
Lions is an imprint of the Children's Division,
part of the Collins Publishing Group
8 Grafton Street, London W1X 3LA

Printed in Great Britain
by William Collins Sons & Co. Ltd, Glasgow
ISBN 0 00 673591 6

CONTENTS

ACKNOWLEDGEMENTS

The author wishes to thank Mary Cadogan and Jessica Yates for having suggested he could write this book and Rosemary Sandberg at Collins for believing them. He is specially indebted to Caroline Thompson for her assiduous picture research and to Ian Butterworth and Heather Garioch for designing the book so elegantly. The writing of the book owes much to those who, over the years, have shared reminiscences of C. S. Lewis: Peter Bide, June and Roger Lancelyn Green, Douglas Gresham and George Sayer; to fellow Lewis enthusiasts Polly March, Dora Brown Marshall, Richard Parlour, Raphael Shaberman, Norman Stone and Geoffrey Marshall Taylor; to Walter Hooper who encouraged him and answered difficult questions; to Pauline Baynes for her valued friendship and for agreeing to revisit Narnia with her paints and brushes; to Alex Platt who translated his scribble into a manuscript and to his ever-patient editor Rosemary Stones who has miraculously turned the whole thing into a book!

The publishers thank the following for their kind permission to reproduce photographs:

The Ancient Art and Architecture Collection, p 85; BBC Enterprises Ltd, p 95 right. Aslan designed and made by Vin Burnham; BBC, p 96 right; Barnaby's Picture Library, p 17 left; Courtesy of Pauline Baynes, p 25; The Bodleian Library, Oxford MS Eng. lett. c.220/1 fol 161, p 76, p 86; Gerald Murray/Vanessa Ford Productions, p 96 left; Charles Jamieson/Vanessa Ford Productions, p 95 left; By permission of the Dean and Chapter of Hereford, p 86; Hulton-Deutsch Collection, p 18 top left, p 23, p 90 left; Courtesy of Richard Lancelyn Green, p 24; The Marion E. Wade Center, Wheaton College, Wheaton, Illinois, USA, p 8, p 9, p 10, p 14, p 17 right, p 18 top right, p 20 top, p 94; Popperfoto, p 20 bottom; Puffin Books, p 18; Punch Publications, p 11 right; Copyright 1947 Time Inc., p 93; The Tale of Squirrel Nutkin by Beatrix Potter, Copyright © Frederick Warne & Co., 1903, Reproduced by permission of Penguin Books Ltd, p 11 bottom; Unwin Hyman, p 25

Every effort has been made to trace the owners of the copyright material in this book. In the event of any questions arising as to use of any material, the Editor will be pleased to make the necessary corrections in future editions of the book.

Do you remember when you first read one of the stories about Narnia and which one it was? I can remember it very well. I was seven and ill in bed with measles, when a friend lent me a copy of *The Lion, the Witch and the Wardrobe* by C. S. Lewis.

I thought it was one of the best books I had ever read – I even tried to climb through the back of my parents' wardrobe – but I got rather frightened when the White Witch did wicked things to Aslan and, I'm ashamed to say, I stopped reading. It was a little while before I discovered how the story really ended and went on to read the rest of the books and, later still, C. S. Lewis's writings for grown-ups.

Now I am writing *this* book for everyone who, like me, enjoys those seven magical volumes that make up The Chronicles of Narnia. You can read about each of the stories and the characters and places in them, as well as the story of C. S. Lewis himself and how he came to create the world beyond the wardrobe door.

Pauline Baynes, who drew the first pictures of Narnia, has made some marvellous new drawings especially for this book, which we both hope you will enjoy looking at and reading. We also hope that when you've done that, you will want to go back to C. S. Lewis's books themselves or, if you only know the stories from seeing them on television or hearing them on radio, that you will now want to read them and discover for yourself the unforgettable Land of Narnia.

Brian Sibley

Jack's mother, Florence Lewis (known to the family as Flora)

LETTERS, letters, letters: C. S. Lewis received hundreds of them every week. Once he had become a famous author, people started writing to him from all over the world. Most of his letters came from grown-ups, but after he started writing children's books in 1950, he also began getting a lot of letters from young people.

When one boy wrote to ask what had inspired him to write his stories, C. S. Lewis replied: "Really I don't know. Does anyone know where exactly an idea comes from?"

The answer to that, of course, is "No"; but, if we look at C. S. Lewis's life, we will see that many of the situations he was to use in his books grew out of the experiences of his early years.

C. S. Lewis was born on 29 November 1898, in Belfast, Northern Ireland. His father, Albert Lewis, was a solicitor and his mother, Flora, was the daughter of a clergyman.

He was christened Clive Staples Lewis, but because he had a brother, Warren, who was three years older, Mr and Mrs Lewis gave Clive the nickname "Baby". Sometimes he was called "Babs" or "Babsie" or "Babbins",

Albert Lewis, Jack's father

but when he was four he decided that he wanted a new name for himself.

His brother later recalled how the young Clive marched up to their mother, "put his forefinger on his chest and announced 'He is Jacksie'". Nobody knows why he chose that particular name, but "on the following day he was still Jacksie, and as he refused absolutely to answer to any other name, Jacksie it had to be". Even when he grew up, C. S. Lewis was always "Jacks" or "Jack" to his family and friends.

The inventive Jack also gave his brother a new name when, as a little boy with the sniffles, he turned to Warren and said: "Warnie wipe nose". And from then on, and for the rest of his life, Warren was known to everyone as Warnie.

The family's Irish nurse, Lizzie Endicott, who looked after the boys, told them wonderful stories about leprechauns and ancient gods. Listening to Lizzie's tales was for Jack the beginning of a lifelong fascination with the extraordinary characters and creatures of myth and legend. Perhaps Jack was thinking of Lizzie when, many years later in *Prince Caspian*, he described how Caspian's nurse told him fabulous tales of Old Narnia.

Five-year-old Jack with one of his favourite toys – Father Christmas riding on a donkey

Little Lea, the Lewis family home from 1905

When Jack was seven, an important event happened. The family moved to a new house called Little Lea. Despite its name, it was a big, rambling house with lots of rooms, stairways and passages. For two imaginative boys it was "less like a house than a city" and when, many years later, Jack wrote the story of his life, he described the "long corridors, empty sunlit rooms, upstair indoor silences, attics explored in solitude, distant noises of gurgling cisterns and pipes and the noise of wind under the tiles". Jack used these memories of Little Lea when he wrote about the attic rooms in the houses where Polly and Digory live in *The Magician's Nephew*.

In one of the many rooms stood a large, carved wardrobe. It had been built out of oak by Jack and Warnie's grandfather, and Warnie remembered how he and his brother used to sit inside in the dark "while Jacks told us tales of adventure". That old wardrobe later gave Jack the idea for a story about how four children found their way into a land called Narnia.

Unfortunately, it was not long after the move to Little Lea that Warnie was sent away to a boarding school in England. Jack missed his brother and, without his best friend, he began to spend more and more time reading

Like Polly in "The Magician's Nephew", Jack used to go up into his secret world in the roof and surround himself with piles of books

books. "In the seemingly endless rainy afternoons," Jack wrote later, "I took volume after volume from the shelves. I had always the same certainty of finding a book that was new to me as a man who walks into a field has of finding a new blade of grass."

Many of the books he read were grown-up novels and biographies, but there were many other good things, like a copy of *Gulliver's Travels* with beautiful colour pictures, and exciting adventures by Mark Twain and Arthur Conan Doyle.

There were also copies of a famous magazine of the day called the *Strand*, which serialized children's stories written by Edith Nesbit, who wrote *Five Children and It* and *The Railway Children*. Jack enjoyed E. Nesbit's stories about how magical things happen to ordinary children and he deliberately tried to capture the same mood when he wrote *The Lion, the Witch and the Wardrobe*.

A "Punch" cartoon by John Tenniel

Mr Lewis had collected bound copies of the humorous magazine *Punch* and, looking through these, Jack discovered the political cartoons of John Tenniel, who also illustrated Lewis Carroll's *Alice's Adventures in Wonderland* and *Through the Looking Glass*. John Tenniel sometimes drew animals dressed up as people to represent different countries and the idea that animals might talk and behave like humans was one that appealed to Jack's vivid imagination.

Beatrix Potter's Squirrel Nutkin

He found the same idea, used rather differently, in the American stories of Brer Rabbit and in the little books written and illustrated by Beatrix Potter, of which Jack's great favourite was *The Tale of Squirrel Nutkin*.

Other books which he enjoyed and which helped influence his own writing were adventure stories like H. Rider Haggard's *King Solomon's Mines* and romantic tales of the Age of Chivalry and knights-in-armour such as Conan Doyle's *Sir Nigel*. Jack said that one of the things he had wished for when he was a boy was a real suit of armour but, he added sadly, "it never came my way". Peter, Edmund, and the other children whom he later sent into Narnia, were much more fortunate.

Because of the books he was reading, it is not too surprising that when Jack began writing stories of his own they were "about chivalrous mice and rabbits who rode out in complete mail to kill not giants but cats".

One of his earliest pieces of invention, probably written in 1906, was a play called *The King's Ring*. Set in Animal-Land in the year 1327, (during the reign of King Bunny the 1st), the play is full of what young Jack (who wasn't very good at spelling) referred to as "interesting carictars" such as a frog field-marshal named Sir Big, Mr Icthus-oress who "made his fortune playing the harp", Sir Goose who was a rich baron and a spy, the King's general called Mr Gold Fish and a brave knight-in-waiting named Sir Peter Mouse.

After inventing the imaginary world of Animal-Land, Jack next began writing a *History of Mouse-Land* and its inhabitants, from the time of Hacom, Chief of the Blue-Bottle tribe to a cruel monarch called King Bublish.

He also wrote several adventures about heroic Sir Peter Mouse who led the armies of Mouse-Land to war and, "after a sharp, short struggle", conquered nearby Cat-Land. Perhaps Jack remembered these Peter Mouse stories when he later created one of Narnia's most memorable characters, the courageous little Reepicheep.

Reepicheep

Next came *The Geography of Animal-Land*, which Jack described as "a dagger-shaped island lying west of the Great Continent". Jack provided details of the cities of Animal-Land such as Figurdied, Whing, Brall, Boot-town and Murry on the Jemima. The Jemima was Animal-Land's largest river; it may have been named after Beatrix Potter's Jemima Puddleduck. There was also information about mountains, railway routes and the various provinces of Animal-Land which included Pig-Land, Squirrel-Land and Fox-Land which exported potatoes.

Sir Peter Mouse and other Animal-Land characters

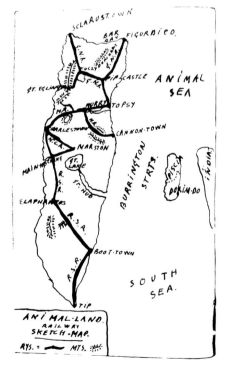

One of Jack's detailed maps for his imaginary country Animal-Land

In 1906, when he was eight, Jack began keeping a record of his life in a diary:

"Pappy is of course the master of the house, and a man in whom you can see the strong Lewis features, bad temper, very sensible, nice when not in a temper. Mamy is like most middle aged ladys, stout, brown hair, spectaciles, knitting her chief industry. I am like most boys of 8 and I am like Papy, bad temper, thick lips, thin, and generally wearing a jersey…Hoora! Warnie comes home this morning. I am lying in bed waiting for him and thinking about him, and before I know where I am I hear his boots pounding on the stairs, he comes into the room, we shake hands and begin to talk…"

There was lots to talk about: Warnie had stories of what it was like to go in a big boat to England and what life was like at school, and Jack could tell his brother how he and Maud, the family maid, had rescued Peter the mouse from "a big BLACK CAT" and about the excitement at Hallowe'en when they had let off "fireworks, rockets, catterine wheels, squbes, and a kind of thing you lit and twirled and then they made STARS".

There were summer holidays together at the seaside and, when the weather was fine, the two boys played in the garden or took bicycle rides into the countryside. But on wet days – of which there seemed to be a lot in Ireland – Jack and Warnie were "forbidden to leave the house under any pretext whatever". When this happened, they went up into the attics and wrote stories and drew pictures.

Jack and Warnie were not just brothers but close friends who did everything together

Lord Big of Boxen drawn by the young Jack

Warnie mostly wrote tales of adventure set in India, and the brothers collaborated to create Boxen, an imaginary realm uniting the fictional Animal-Land and the real India into one continent.

In 1908, a terrible blow hit Jack and Warnie. Their mother was found to be suffering from cancer. Ten-year-old Jack, who was frightened by his mother's illness and by the coming and going of doctors and nurses, often during the night, decided he would pray to God and ask him to make her better. When that did not happen, Jack believed God had let him down.

Although he later came to believe very strongly in a God who cared about people who had problems or were in pain, Jack never forgot the great sadness that he and Warnie experienced during their mother's illness. He eventually drew on that memory when he described Digory in *The Magician's Nephew* trying to find a cure for his dying mother.

Digory and his mother

In the story, of course, Digory is helped by Aslan and his mother does get better. In real life, Jack's mother did not recover, and when she eventually died he felt as if "all settled happiness, all that was tranquil and reliable" had been taken away.

Only days after Mrs Lewis died, Jack was packed off to England with Warnie to go to school. It was the first of several schools he was to attend over the next few years, but at all of them he was unhappy.

Life at boarding school in those days was not always very pleasant: junior boys had to act as servants for the older boys and they were regularly beaten for doing even the smallest things wrong.

Jack escaped into a world of books and, having read some science-fiction stories by H. G. Wells, he began writing an action-packed story about a trip to Mars.

Arthur Rackham's illustration of Siegfried killing Fafnir the dragon

He also discovered a much older form of fantasy when, in 1911, he came across a copy of the German legend of *Siegfried and the Twilight of the Gods* with pictures by the illustrator Arthur Rackham. Jack fell under the spell of these stories of dwarves, dragons, magic rings and enchanted swords and his pleasure was complete when he later heard Richard Wagner's powerful music inspired by the tales. Jack began to read all the books he could find about the old German legends and the myths of the gods and heroes of the Norsemen.

After an unhappy year at his last school, Malvern College, Jack's father sent him to a private tutor, W. T. Kirkpatrick, so that he could study for an entrance examination to Oxford University. Kirk, as his teacher was nicknamed, encouraged Jack to read and find out about things for himself.

Jack paid a special tribute to his tutor when, years later, he wrote *The Lion, the Witch and the Wardrobe*. The old man in whose house the children find a doorway into Narnia is called Professor Kirke.

During the two years that Jack lived and studied with W. T. Kirkpatrick he learnt several languages. He also wrote one or two stories, and lots of poetry, and he continued to read and read.

One of the authors he read for the first time was George MacDonald, who wrote *At the Back of the North Wind* and other well-known books for children. It was on a railway station bookstall that Jack found Macdonald's novel *Phantastes*, a story about a young man's journey into fairyland. It made a great impact on Jack and influenced his own writing, especially the tales of Narnia.

Jack began his studies at University College, Oxford in 1917, but, just five months later, he went to France as a second lieutenant to fight in the First World War. The following year he was hit by a piece of shrapnel, wounded and sent back to England. Warnie, who had joined up before Jack, remained in the army after the war was over and became a major.

Jack (left) boating with his friend Paddy Moore who was killed in the First World War

Magdalen College, Oxford

In 1919, Jack returned to his studies in Oxford and in the same year published his first book, a collection of poems. Over the next four years he sat and passed all his examinations with distinction.

When he had finished his education, Jack decided to stay on in Oxford and work as a tutor. In 1925 he went to teach at Magdalen College, where he remained until 1954 when he went as a professor to a college of the same name in Britain's other famous university town, Cambridge.

Among the many friends Jack made in Oxford was J. R. R. Tolkien who later wrote *The Hobbit* and *The Lord of the Rings*. Although Tolkien's stories are very different from The Chronicles of Narnia, they are just as exciting and imaginative. Together with Tolkien and a number of other writers, Jack started The Inklings, an informal club which met to talk and tell one another stories.

As well as a great storyteller, J. R. R. Tolkien was also a very religious man, and it was partly as a result of his friendship that Jack began to think about his feelings towards Christianity.

He became a Christian in 1929, and within four years had written his first religious book, *The Pilgrim's Regress*. Inspired by John Bunyan's famous story *The Pilgrim's Progress*, it told how Jack had come to believe in God.

J. R. R. Tolkien and (below) the book that made him famous. The cover for this edition of "The Hobbit" was designed by Pauline Baynes

Jack's fondness for fantasy and his strong religious beliefs resulted in his writing *Out of the Silent Planet*, a science-fiction novel about a Christian and two evil men who travel in a spaceship to Mars and become involved with the mysterious creatures that live there. Jack went on to write two more science-fiction books, *Perelandra or Voyage to Venus* and *That Hideous Strength*.

During the Second World War, Jack began a new career as a broadcaster for the BBC as well as writing several new books on Christianity including *The Screwtape Letters* in which a senior devil gives advice on how to deal with human beings to Wormwood, his young, inexperienced, nephew. And it was around this time that Jack began thinking about writing a book for children. But what happened next is another story...

THE one question C. S. Lewis was asked more than any other was "How did you write The Chronicles of Narnia?" When, towards the end of his life, he tried to answer that question for a magazine, he began with a warning: "You must not believe all that authors tell you about how they wrote their books. This is not because they mean to tell lies. It is because a man writing a story is too excited about the story itself to sit back and notice how he is doing it. In fact, that might stop the works; just as, if you start thinking about how you tie your tie, the next thing is that you find you can't tie it…"

Perhaps the best reason Jack Lewis ever gave for writing his children's books was when he said, "People won't write the books I want, so I have to do it for myself…"

Some writers – like Lewis Carroll, Kenneth Grahame and Jack's friend J. R. R. Tolkien – wrote their stories for particular children. But, unlike Tolkien and Kenneth Grahame, Jack was a bachelor and he didn't have any children; and, unlike Lewis Carroll, he didn't go out of his way to make friends with children. In fact, Jack very seldom met any young people and, when he did, he usually felt rather awkward with them.

Writing to his god-daughter, Sarah, whom he hadn't seen for years, Jack told her that if they were to meet she would find him "very shy and dull". Then he added: "By the way, always remember that old people can be quite as shy with young people as young people can be with old. This explains what must seem to you the idiotic way in which so many grown-ups talk to you."

This tells us something very important about Jack: although he had no children of his own, he never quite forgot what it was like to be a child. "I don't think," he once said, "that age matters so much as people think. Parts of me are still twelve and I think other parts were already fifty when I was twelve…"

Then, in 1939, something happened which helped him begin to enjoy the company of children. Britain was at war, and because bombs were being dropped on London, as many children as possible were sent to live in the country for safety.

Four young evacuees came to stay with Jack at his Oxford home, The Kilns

Normally, children wouldn't have been sent to live with a forty-year-old unmarried man, but Jack and Warnie (who had been recalled to the army) shared their house with an elderly lady called Mrs Moore.

Jack had been a friend of Mrs Moore's son, Paddy, 26 years earlier, when they were soldiers together in the First World War. Jack had promised that if anything happened to Paddy, he would look after Mrs Moore; and when Paddy was killed in action, she became a kind of "adopted mother" to Jack and lived with him and Warnie for the rest of her life.

Children leaving London for the country during the war

And that is how it happened that the first of several groups of evacuees (as the children sent away from London were called) came to live in Jack's Oxford home. "I never appreciated children," he later wrote to a friend, "till the war brought them to me."

As Jack got to know the evacuee children, he was sad to find how little they read and how few imaginative stories they seemed to know. He seems to have suddenly got the idea of writing a story for young readers, because one day, when he was working on one of his adult books, he quickly scribbled down some opening sentences on the back of one of the pages:

This book is about four children whose names were Ann, Martin, Rose and Peter. But is is mostly about Peter who was the youngest. They all had to go away from London suddenly because of the Air Raids, and because Father, who was in the Army, had gone off to the War and Mother was doing some kind of war work. They were sent to stay with a relation of Mother's who was a very old Professor who lived by himself in the country…

And that was as far as the story went, although another very important part of the idea came into his head about this time. One of the girls asked Jack if there was anything *behind* the old wardrobe which stood in The Kilns. The question started him thinking, and he remembered how when he and Warnie were young they used to climb inside their grandfather's wardrobe and tell each other tales in the dark. He may also have half-remembered reading, as a child, E. Nesbit's 1908 short story *The Aunt and Amabel*, in which an enchanted world is reached via 'Bigwardrobeinspareroom'…

Edmund finds his way into Narnia

Sometimes a writer's ideas take a long while to come to anything and Jack was so busy that he never seemed to have the time to work on his children's story. It wasn't until nine years later, in 1948, that Jack told a friend that he was thinking of writing a children's book in the tradition of E. Nesbit.

When, in 1960, the BBC broadcast a radio serial of *The Lion, the Witch and the Wardrobe*, the magazine *Radio Times* invited Jack to tell listeners how he came to write the book. It began, he wrote, "with pictures in my head. At first they were not a story, just pictures. The *Lion* began with a picture of a faun carrying an umbrella and parcels in a snowy wood. This picture had been in my mind since I was about sixteen. Then one day, when I was about forty," (actually, he was nearly fifty) "I said to myself: 'Let's try and make a story about it.'" Two other pictures were to become an important part of that story: "a queen on a sledge" and "a magnificent lion".

As to where the pictures *came from*, Jack always said he didn't know. At first he had little or no idea how the story was going to develop, "But then, suddenly, Aslan came bounding in. I think I had been having a good many dreams of lions about that time. Apart from that, I don't know where the Lion came from or why he came. But once He was there, He pulled the whole story together..."

And so, with these pictures in his head, Jack began inventing. In his first attempt to begin the story, Jack had called his characters Ann, Martin, Rose and Peter. Now the story began: "Once there were four children whose names were Peter, Susan, Edmund and Lucy..."

Jack probably kept the name "Peter" because, as you will remember, that had been the name of the mouse hero in his Boxon stories. The name "Lucy" was borrowed from someone Jack knew. Lucy was the daughter of his friend Owen Barfield and Jack was her godfather.

C. S. Lewis

"When I was ten," Jack wrote in 1952, "I read fairy tales in secret and would have been ashamed if I had been found doing so. Now that I am fifty, I read them openly. When I became a man I put away childish things, including the fear of childishness and the desire to be very grown-up."

Which explains what he says to Lucy Barfield in the front of *The Lion, the Witch and the Wardrobe:*

My Dear Lucy,

I wrote this story for you, but when I began it I had not realized that girls grow quicker than books. As a result you are already too old for fairy tales, and by the time it is printed and bound you will be older still. But some day you will be old enough to start reading fairy tales again. You can then take it down from some upper shelf, dust it and tell me what you think of it. I shall probably be too deaf to hear, and too old to understand, a word you say, but I shall still be
your affectionate Godfather,
C. S. Lewis

As Jack wrote his book he began including mythical characters from the old tales he had enjoyed as a boy, although these almost caused the book to be abandoned when he showed what he was writing to his friend J. R. R. Tolkien. Much to Jack's disappointment, Tolkien was very critical of the story and particularly the inclusion in the new world of Narnia of not only creatures from classical mythology but also Father Christmas.

Tolkien also felt that Jack had rather dashed the story off without giving to it anything like the same time and care he himself was taking in creating Middle-Earth, the land in *The Hobbit* and *The Lord of the Rings*. Perhaps Tolkien was even a little jealous of how quickly Jack was able to write compared with the length of time it took him to write his stories.

Anyway, Jack was so discouraged by Tolkien's criticisms that he put the story to one side for a while. Then, some time later, he looked at it again and started rewriting the first few chapters.

But Jack was still very unsure whether the story was any good. Fortunately for us, he decided to ask the advice of another friend, Roger Lancelyn Green, who was later to write and edit lots of children's books of his own.

One evening, in his room in Magdalen College, Jack read Roger the first two chapters of *The Lion*. Suddenly he stopped and asked: "Do you think it's worth going on with?" Without hesitation, his friend told him that it was.

"As he read," Roger Lancelyn Green later remembered, "there had crept over me a feeling of awe and excitement: not only that it was better than most children's books which were appearing at the time – but the conviction that I was listening to the first reading of a great classic."

With Roger's encouragement, Jack completed the book and began to think about illustrations. At first he thought he might draw his own pictures (just as he had done for his Boxon stories) but eventually

Roger Lancelyn Green he decided the book would need the talents of a professional artist.

An illustration by Pauline Baynes from J. R. R. Tolkien's "Farmer Giles of Ham"

Jack found exactly the right artist when he saw the illustrations that had just been completed for Tolkien's new book, *Farmer Giles of Ham*. The pictures included lots of birds and animals – as well as a quite splendid dragon – which suggested that the artist, Pauline Baynes, might be the person to draw the variety of creatures to be found in *The Lion, the Witch and the Wardrobe*.

Pauline Baynes was in her mid-twenties when Jack's publisher commissioned her to produce what was to be the first of several hundred wonderfully detailed illustrations to The Chronicles of Narnia. It was to be a happy partnership of two highly gifted people; and Jack never tried to tell the young artist how to interpret his stories (apart from the odd occasion when she got something wrong, such as showing a boat being rowed backwards or someone with a shield on the wrong arm).

Jack finished writing *The Lion, the Witch and the Wardrobe* in March 1949, but it was not published until the following year. By this time, he had written two more stories about the Land of Narnia.

Three months after finishing *The Lion*, Jack read Roger Lancelyn Green the opening pages to a sequel. It was the story of a boy called Digory:

Pauline Baynes at the time she was illustrating the Narnia books and (below) in 1973

Digory went straight up to the big Oak and said, "Hullo, Oak." And immediately the Oak, with a creaking, oaken kind of voice, replied, "Hullo, Digory."

If an oak said anything to you or me we should be very surprised; in fact we should either feel rather frightened or think we were dreaming. But Digory was not surprised at all, for it had been happening to him all his life... Ever since he could remember he had had the gift of being able to understand the trees and flowers...

Polly and Digory

Digory can also talk to the birds and animals and he has a conversation with Pattertwig, a red squirrel, who gives him a walnut to eat out of his winter store.

But Digory loses his magical powers when he cuts off one of the Oak's branches to help Polly, the girl next door, make a raft she is building to explore the stream at the bottom of her garden.

Then Digory, who lives with his Aunt Gertrude, receives a visit from his godmother, the mysterious Mrs Lefay, who appears to be a kind of sorceress and carries a rabbit called Coiny in her bag. Mrs Lefay invites Digory to see her and gives the boy directions on how to find "a furniture shop that sells birds and pictures".

Once there, Mrs Lefay tells Digory, "You must go into the shop and you will see…"

What Digory would have seen we will never know, because Jack never wrote any more of the story. Digory and Polly, of course, later became the central characters in *The Magician's Nephew*, and Mrs Lefay was what Jack called Uncle Andrew's bad fairy-godmother. The name "Lefay" comes from the legends of King Arthur in which the evil sorceress is named Morgan le Fay; in fact "fay" is another word for "fairy".

Digory's Aunt Gertrude seems to have become the model for the frightful Head Teacher of Experiment House, the school attended by Jill and Eustace in *The Silver Chair*. Rather like that lady, Aunt Gertrude "had been a schoolmistress and bullied girls. Then she became a headmistress and bullied the mistresses. Then she became an inspector and bullied headmistresses. Then she went into Parliament and became a Minister of something and bullied everybody."

As for Pattertwig the squirrel, he was to appear in the very next Narnian story…

Pattertwig

Like *The Lion*, the later Chronicles of Narnia began with pictures. In one of his notebooks around this time, Jack jotted down some possible "PLOTS":

SHIP. Two children somehow got on board a ship of ancient build. Discover presently that they are sailing in time (backwards): the captain will bring them to islands that have not existed for millennia – *(millennia means a period of several thousand years)* – Approach islands. Attack by enemies. Children captured. Discover that the first captain was really taking them because his sick King needs blood of a boy in the far future. *Nevertheless* prefer the capt. and his side to their… rescuers. Escape and return to their first hosts. The blood giving, not fatal, and happy ending. Various islands… can be thrown in. Beauty of the ship the initial spell. To be a v. green and pearly story.
PICTURE. A magic picture. One of the children gets thro' the frame into the picture and one of the creatures gets out of the picture into our world.
SEQUEL TO L.W.W. The present tyrants to be Men. Intervening history of Narnia told nominally by the Dwarf…

The "Dawn Treader"

The picture (which may have been inspired by an episode in John Masefield's children's book *The Box of Delights*) and the ship are obviously early ideas for *The Voyage of the "Dawn Treader"*. But before that story was written, Jack decided to follow up his other idea and tell his readers what had happened in Narnia after the events told in *The Lion*.

That story, which is mostly about young Prince Caspian, is told to Peter, Susan, Edmund and Lucy who have been magically transported back to Narnia from a railway station in England. The children hear the story – which takes up four chapters of the book – from

Trumpkin

Trumpkin the dwarf, but, wrote Jack, "I shall not give it to you in his words, putting in all the children's questions and interruptions, because it would take too long and be confusing…"

The book was first going to be called *Drawn into Narnia*, but when Jack's publisher said that he didn't like the title, it was changed to *A Horn in Narnia* and then to *Prince Caspian* with the subtitle *The Return to Narnia*.

Jack found *Prince Caspian* much harder to write than *The Lion*, but eventually it was completed and Pauline Baynes was once again asked to do the pictures. The pictures that she drew for *Prince Caspian* and for all the Chronicles, have become as much a part of the books as the stories themselves.

Prince Caspian

After *Prince Caspian*, which was published in 1951, Jack went back to his story ideas about the ship and the magic picture and wrote *The Voyage of the "Dawn Treader"*, which appeared in the bookshops in 1952. This time only Edmund and Lucy return to Narnia accompanied by the delightfully obnoxious Eustace Scrubb.

"When I had done *The Voyage*," Jack wrote to a young friend, "I felt quite sure it would be the last. But I found I was wrong…" The next story was set during the years described at the end of *The Lion* when Peter, Susan, Edmund and Lucy were Kings and Queens of Narnia. It began as *Narnia and the North*, but several other titles were considered such as *The Desert Road to Narnia, Cor of Archenland, Over the Border, The Horse Bree* and *The Horse Stole the Boy*.

Eventually the story of Shasta of Calormen and the talking horse, Bree, was published in 1954 as *The Horse and His Boy*. But before the growing number of Narnian readers saw *that* story they were to read another one.

The new story was about how Eustace and a schoolfriend, Jill Pole, get into Narnia and rescue Prince Rilian from the terrible Queen of Underland. Jack wanted to call the book *The Wild Waste Lands*, but when his publisher turned that down he began to look for an alternative title. Roger Lancelyn Green suggested *Night Under Narnia*, but

Jill, Eustace and Puddleglum

that was felt to be too gloomy; so was Jack's next suggestion, *Gnomes Under Narnia*, and the book was then almost called *News under Narnia*. It finally appeared, in 1953, as *The Silver Chair*, the book that introduced readers to one of the most delightful and loved Narnian characters, Puddleglum the Marsh-wiggle.

For his sixth book, Jack turned to the story he had begun to write a few years before, just after completing *The Lion*. In *Polly and Digory*, as it was first called, Jack went back in time many years to tell how Aslan had created the Land of Narnia and how and why people from our world had become involved in its history.

As the story developed, Jack also found a way of ex-

The last battle for Narnia

plaining some of the curious things in *The Lion, the Witch and the Wardrobe*, such as what a London lamp-post was doing in the woods of Narnia, where the White Witch came from, why it was that Professor Kirke believed the children's incredible story about the land beyond the wardrobe and how the wardrobe itself came to have such amazing magical powers.

The book was published, with the title *The Magician's Nephew*, in 1955, and by that time Jack had finished writing the last book in the series. When it was "still only in pen-and-ink", Jack told a young friend that he had not quite decided what to call it. "Sometimes," he said, "I think of calling it *The Last King of Narnia* and sometimes *Night Falls on Narnia*. Which do you think sounds best?"

The title finally chosen for the seventh story of Narnia, published in 1956, was *The Last Battle*, and in it Jack completed his stories by telling how Narnia comes to an end and what happens to everyone afterwards.

It was Roger Lancelyn Green who suggested Jack should call the series The Chronicles of Narnia, which is how they've been known ever since.

Now that the last Narnia book was finished, Jack carefully worked out a chronology to show how Narnian and English time relate to one another. On Jack's chart (opposite) you will see that Aslan created Narnia in the English year 1900 and that one thousand years passed before the four children found their way there through the wardrobe in 1940. There were then another 1555 years before the last battle and the end of Narnia.

C. S. Lewis's Outline of Narnian History
so far as it is known

Narnian years

English years

1   *Creation of Narnia. The Beasts made able to talk. Digory plants the Tree of Protection. The White Witch Jadis enters Narnia but flies into the far North. Frank I becomes King of Narnia.*

180   *Prince Col, younger son of King Frank V of Narnia, leads certain followers into Archenland (not then inhabited) and becomes first King of that country.*

204   *Certain outlaws from Archenland fly across the Southern desert and set up the new kindom of Calormen.*

300   *The empire of Calormen spreads mightily. Calormenes colonize the land of Telmar to the West of Narnia.*

302   *The Calormenes in Telmar behave very wickedly and Aslan turns them into dumb beasts. The country lies waste. King Gale of Narnia delivers the Lone Islands from a dragon and is made Emperor by their grateful inhabitants.*

407   *Olvin of Archenland kills the Giant Pire.*

460   *Pirates from our world take possession of Telmar.*

570   *About this time lived Moonwood the Hare.*

898   *The White Witch Jadis returns into Narnia out of the far North.*

900   *The long winter begins*

1000   *The Pevensies arrive in Narnia. The treachery of Edmund. The sacrifice of Aslan. The White Witch defeated and the Long Winter ended. Peter becomes High King of Narnia.*

1014   *King Peter carries out a successful raid on the Northern Giants. Queen Susan and King Edmund visit the Court of Calormen. King Lune of Archenland discovers his long-lost son Prince Cor and defeats a treacherous attack by Prince Rabadash of Calormen.*

1015   *The Pevensies hunt the White Stag and vanish out of Narnia.*

1050   *Ram the Great succeeds Cor as King of Archenland.*

1502   *About this time lived Queen Swanwhite of Narnia.*

1998   *The Telmarines invade and conquer Narina. Caspian I becomes King of Narnia.*

2290   *Prince Caspian, son of Caspian IX, born. Caspian IX murdered by his brother Miraz who usurps the throne.*

2303   *Prince Caspian escapes from his uncle Miraz. Civil War in Narnia. By the aid of Aslan and of the Pevensies, whom Caspian summons with Queen Susan's magic Horn, Miraz is defeated and killed. Caspian becomes King Caspian X of Narnia.*

2304   *Caspian X defeats the Northern Giants.*

2306-7   *Caspian X's great voyage to the end of the World.*

2310   *Caspian X marries Ramandu's daughter.*

2325   *Prince Rilian born.*

2345   *The Queen killed by a Serpent. Rilian disappears.*

2356   *Eustace and Jill appear in Narnia and rescue Prince Rilian. Death of Caspian X.*

2534   *Outbreak of outlaws in Lantern Waste. Towers built to guard that region.*

2555   *Rebellion of Shift the Ape. King Tirian rescued by Eustace and Jill. Narnia in the hands of the Calormenes. The last battle. End of Narnia. End of the World.*

In 1957 a boy called Laurence wrote to C. S. Lewis to ask in what order he should read The Chronicles of Narnia. Laurence's mother thought he should read them in the order in which they were published; Laurence himself thought he should begin with *The Magician's Nephew* and then read *The Lion, the Witch and the Wardrobe*, *The Horse and His Boy*, *Prince Caspian*, *The Voyage of the "Dawn Treader"*, *The Silver Chair* and *The Last Battle*.

"I think," wrote the author in reply, "I agree with your order for reading the books more than with your mother's..." So that is the order I follow here. And after summarising each story I give an account of what else is known of Narnian history at that time.

The Magician's Nephew

"This is... a very important story," wrote C. S. Lewis, "because it shows how all the comings and goings between our own world and the land of Narnia first began."

It is the year 1900 and twelve-year-old Digory Kirke and his sick mother are living with relatives in London because Digory's father is away in India.

Digory makes friends with a girl called Polly Plummer who lives next door and they go exploring in the attics at the top of their houses. By mistake they enter a room used by Digory's Uncle Andrew, who is a magician and in the middle of a strange experiment.

Polly and Digory awaken the terrible Queen Jadis

Uncle Andrew tricks Polly into putting on a magic ring and she disappears. Then he makes Digory take a ring and go after her with two other rings to bring them both home.

Uncle Andrew began his experiments by using magic rings to send guinea pigs into another world

Digory suddenly finds himself in a wood with lots of pools among the trees. Polly is already there, but the wood is enchanted and they both grow so sleepy and forgetful it looks as if they won't ever get away.

Once they *have* found out how to get back home again, they decide to explore some of the other pools. The first one they try takes them to the ruined city of Charn. The place seems deserted until they find a great hall with a long line of seated figures of kings and queens.

In the middle of the hall is a bell and a hammer. Digory rings the bell and the last figure in the room comes to life. It is Jadis, Queen of Charn.

Jadis shows Polly and Digory her kingdom which is now in ruins and tells them her history: how she fought her sister for the throne and, when all else failed, how she used the Deplorable Word – "The secret of secrets…a word which if spoken with the proper ceremonies, would destroy all living things except the one who spoke it."

Jadis demands that Digory take her back to his world, but the children escape using the magic rings. When they reach the Wood between the Worlds they find that Jadis is with them and fast losing her powers.

The children jump into their "home" pool but Jadis manages to hold on to Digory and all three of them arrive in Uncle Andrew's attic.

Jadis causes havoc in London: she steals and crashes a hansom cab and then starts a street brawl, wrenching the crossbars off a lamp-post as a weapon.

Using the magic rings, Digory and Polly attempt to get her back to Charn, but they find they have not only taken Jadis out of London but also Uncle Andrew, the cab driver and his horse, Strawberry.

Then, by accident, they all get into yet another world where, at first, there seems to be nothing at all. But out of the darkness a voice begins to sing a wonderful song. The singer is a great Lion and it sings a creation song. As the Lion paces to and fro in the land, singing, sun and stars, trees and flowers come into being, and birds and animals are born out of the earth.

Jadis tries to stop the Lion by hurling the bar from the lamp-post at him, but the Lion is unharmed and the Queen runs for her life. Where the iron bar falls, a lamp-post begins to grow.

Uncle Andrew runs for his life

Then the Lion, who is Aslan, calls his new world to life: "Narnia, Narnia, Narnia, awake. Love. Think. Speak. Be walking trees. Be talking beasts. Be divine waters." Aslan chooses two of each animal – among them Strawberry the cab horse – and gives them the power of speech. While the talking animals have great fun with the terrified Uncle Andrew, Digory and Polly have to explain to Aslan about Jadis and the trouble they have brought into Narnia.

Aslan invites the cabby, whose name is Frank, to stay and become King and, when he accepts, the Lion brings Frank's wife from London to Narnia.

Then Aslan sends Digory on an errand. He is to travel beyond the Western Wilds to a garden on a hill. There he is to pick an apple and return with it to Aslan. To take Digory on his journey, Aslan gives Strawberry a great pair of wings and a new name, Fledge.

Polly offers to go with Digory and astride the flying horse the two children set off. When at last they reach the garden Digory reads an inscription on the gates:

Digory and Polly astride Fledge

Come in by the gold gates or not at all,
Take of my fruit for others or forbear,
For those who steal or those who climb my wall
Shall find their heart's desire and find despair.

Inside he finds the tree and picks the apple. Digory is tempted to eat one himself but then he notices a strange bird watching him from the branches. Then he sees Jadis in the garden eating one of the apples. She tells him to forget Aslan and to take the fruit home to his mother who will be made better if she eats it.

Digory refuses to do what Jadis says and he and Polly fly back to Narnia on Fledge. Aslan tells Digory to plant the apple and from it there at once grows up a tree that will protect Narnia from the evil Jadis.

After the cabby and his wife have been crowned King Frank and Queen Helen of Narnia, Aslan gives Digory an apple from the new tree to take home to his mother.

(opposite)
Digory picks
the fruit in the
magic garden

Aslan sends Digory, Polly and Uncle Andrew back to London, having given the children orders to bury the magic rings when they get back to their world.

Digory gives his mother the Narnian apple and she begins to get better; then he buries the apple core, together with the magic rings, in the garden. The tree which eventually grows from that apple is more like a Narnian tree than one from this world.

Digory's mother recovers and his father returns from India and they all go to live in the country. When, many years later, the apple tree in the London garden is blown down in a storm, Digory Kirke (who is now a Professor) has the tree made into a wardrobe…

The Coronation of King Frank and Queen Helen

One hundred and eighty Narnian years after Aslan created the land, Prince Col, the youngest son of King Frank and Queen Helen, goes south to Archenland with some followers and becomes its first king. Twenty-four years later, a group of outlaws leave Archenland, cross the southern desert and establish the new kingdom of Calormen.

By the year 300, the Calormen empire has grown and the Calormenes make a colony from the land of Telmar to the west of Narnia, but do such wicked things that Aslan turns them into dumb animals. The same year, King Gale of Narnia rescues the Lone Islands from a dragon and becomes the Islands' Emperor.

Over 450 years pass and pirates from our world get into Narnia and take over Telmar. Then in 898 Jadis returns as the White Witch. After two years there begins the Long Winter…

The Lion, The Witch And The Wardrobe

It is 1940 and England is at war. Professor Digory Kirke (who forty years earlier had witnessed the creation of Narnia) lives in a big house in the country. In one room is the wardrobe made from a tree grown from a Narnian apple...

Because of the air-raids on London, Peter, Susan, Edmund and Lucy Pevensie (their last name, by the way, isn't ever used in *this* story) are sent to live with Professor Kirke.

The house was the sort "that you never seem to come to the end of, and was full of unexpected places", so the children soon go exploring. One of the rooms they visit is empty except for a wardrobe... When Peter, Susan and Edmund leave the room, Lucy stays behind to look inside.

The wardrobe is full of fur coats, but when Lucy climbs in, the fur coats magically turn into fir trees and Lucy finds she is walking on snow.

Lucy is in a snow-covered wood and among the trees stands a lamp-post. Then Lucy meets a faun (who has

the body of a man and the horns and legs of a goat), carrying parcels and an umbrella. The faun tells Lucy his name is Tumnus and that she is in the Land of Narnia.

Mr Tumnus asks Lucy to his home for tea and, after they have eaten, he plays some strange music on his pipes which makes Lucy feel sleepy. Suddenly the faun stops playing and begins to cry. Mr Tumnus tells Lucy that he is a spy for the White Witch and has an order to keep watch for any sons of Adam or Daughters of Eve in Narnia. It is the Witch, he tells Lucy, who "has got all of Narnia under her thumb. It's she that makes it always winter. Always winter and never Christmas…"

What *we* now know, but Lucy didn't (and C. S. Lewis didn't know either when he wrote this story), is that although it is only forty English years since Digory and Polly were in Narnia, a thousand years have passed in Narnia; and, for the last hundred the land has been ruled by the White Witch who was once Jadis, Queen of Charn.

Mr Tumnus

Mr Tumnus decides not to betray Lucy to the Witch and he returns her safely to the lamp-post. Lucy finds her way back into the wardrobe and hurries to tell her sister and brothers of her adventure. Because Lucy hasn't been missing for any time at all, they don't believe her story and when she insists they examine the wardrobe, all they find inside is fur coats. Poor Lucy is terribly upset.

A few days later, when they are playing hide-and-seek, Lucy climbs into the wardrobe again and, this time, Edmund follows her. Lucy visits Mr Tumnus but Edmund meets someone very different. Riding on a reindeer-drawn sledge, driven by a dwarf, is a great lady dressed in white fur, wearing a crown and carrying a golden wand. "Her face was white – not merely pale, but white like snow…except for her very red mouth."

(opposite)
Lucy meets
Mr Tumnus by
the lamp-post

The White Witch, for that is who she is, finds out about Susan, Lucy and Peter and learns that Lucy has visited Mr Tumnus. By giving Edmund large quantities of the most wonderful Turkish Delight and by promising to make him prince of Narnia, she gets him to agree to bring his brother and sisters to her castle.

After the Witch has gone, Edmund finds Lucy and they go back to the wardrobe. Lucy tells the others that she and Edmund have both been to Narnia, but Edmund denies it and Lucy is even more upset.

Eventually, all four children get into Narnia and go to look for Mr Tumnus, but he is gone and his home is wrecked. Then, in the woods, they see a robin who leads them to a Beaver who has been looking out for them.

Mr Beaver

Mr Beaver takes the children to his house on a dam in the river where Mrs Beaver prepares a meal for them. Following dinner, Mr and Mrs Beaver tell the children more about the White Witch and about the rumours of Aslan's return to Narnia. It is then that they discover that Edmund has gone...

After a terrible journey, Edmund arrives at the Witch's castle which is full of the figures of her enemies whom she has turned into stone. The Witch is angry because Edmund has not brought Susan, Peter and Lucy with him.

The Witch sends the captain of her secret police, a wolf named Maugrim (or, as he is called in American editions of the book, Fenris Ulf) to find the other children before they can meet Aslan. Then, taking the miserable Edmund with her, the Witch sets out in her sledge for the place where the children are bound to be heading – the Stone Table.

Edmund and the White Witch

Realising they have been betrayed, Peter, Lucy and Susan, together with the Beavers, also set out for the Stone Table. On the way they meet Father Christmas who gives them gifts: for Peter, a sword and shield; for Susan, a bow and arrows and a magic horn; and for Lucy, a dagger and a small bottle of healing cordial. Father Christmas tells them, "Aslan is on the move. The Witch's magic is weakening."

Children often asked Jack what happened to the merry-makers who were turned to stone. "I thought," he wrote to one girl, "people would take it for granted that Aslan would put it all right. I see now I should have said so."

Winter begins to give way to spring and soon the Witch is finding it difficult to drive her sledge. Then she comes across a group of animals having a party with food and drink given them by Father Christmas. To Edmund's horror she turns them all into stone.

The children at last meet Aslan, the Lion, "the King of the Wood and son of the great Emperor-beyond-the-Sea". Aslan is showing Peter the Castle of Cair Paravel, where he is to be High King of Narnia, when Maugrim attacks Aslan's camp.

It is Peter's first battle and he rescues Susan and kills the wolf. Aslan knights Peter and sends his people to rescue Edmund, who is about to be killed by the Witch.

Arriving at Aslan's camp, the Witch demands Edmund's life, because under the Emperor's laws, he is a traitor. But Aslan makes a deal with the Witch and gives himself up in Edmund's place. The Witch has the great Lion bound and shaved and then, encouraged by the terrible demons and monsters who are her servants, the Witch kills Aslan with a stone knife on the Stone Table.

The execution of Aslan

The Witch and her supporters leave the place of execution and Susan and Lucy sit with Aslan's body. During the night, some mice gnaw through Aslan's ropes.

The next morning, just as the sun is coming up, the Stone Table breaks in two and the girls see Aslan alive and well again. He explains:

Mice (Jack's favourite animals) gnaw through Aslan's ropes

"Though the Witch knew the Deep Magic, there is a magic deeper still which she did not know. Her knowledge goes back only to the dawn of time. But if she could have looked a little further back, into the stillness and darkness before Time dawned, she would have… known that when a willing victim who has committed no treachery was killed in a traitor's stead, the Table would crack and Death itself would start working backwards."

Lucy and Susan ride with Aslan to the Witch's castle where the Lion breathes on the stone statues and brings them back to life. Lucy is reunited with Mr Tumnus.

When they all return to camp they find Aslan's people battling with the Witch who is turning many of her enemies to stone. Edmund bravely fights with her and breaks her wand, although in doing so he is badly wounded. Then Aslan enters the fight, destroys the Witch and the battle is over.

When Edmund has been healed and has put things right with Aslan, they go to Cair Paravel where Aslan crowns the four children Kings and Queens of Narnia.

Their reign lasts for fifteen years; then one day, while they are out hunting the White Stag who gives wishes, they discover a lamp-post in the wood and their way back into the wardrobe and our world. They have returned only seconds after they left.

This story, which happens during the reign of King Peter and the others, opens in the country of Calormen where a boy named Shasta lives with Arsheesh, an old fisherman whom Shasta thinks is his father.

One day a magnificently-dressed stranger arrives at the fisherman's cottage on a handsome great horse. He is a Tarkaan, or great lord, from the South. The Tarkaan stays the night and, overheard by Shasta, offers to buy the boy from Arsheesh. Shasta learns that the fisherman is not his father but had found him, as a baby, washed ashore in a boat.

Shasta is worried about the idea of becoming the Tarkaan's slave: if only he knew what kind of man the great lord was. If only the Tarkaan's horse could talk, he might tell him. And then, an amazing thing happens: the horse speaks to the boy.

The horse tells Shasta he is a Talking Horse from Narnia who was captured when he was young. His name is Breehy-hinny-brinny-hoohy-hah, but he agrees to let the boy call him Bree.

Bree suggests that they run away together and they

gallop off into the night, heading North towards the city of Tashbaan and then, beyond the desert, to Archenland and the mountain pass into Narnia. "Think of it," says Bree. "To Narnia and the North!"

Shasta and Bree

After they have travelled several weeks, there comes a night when they hear another horse coming up behind them. Then they hear something alarming: the roar of a lion – or, maybe, *two* lions...

Eventually, the two horses are riding side by side and, when they have escaped the lions, Shasta and Bree find their companions are a girl from Calormen called Aravis and her Talking Horse from Narnia, Hwin,

Aravis

Aravis tells Shasta her story: when her mother died, her father remarried but his new wife hated Aravis and arranged for her step-daughter to marry an old man named Ahoshta. Aravis had been on the point of killing herself when she hears her horse speak to her.

Hwin told her about Narnia and they had agreed to run away. By a series of cunning deceptions and by drugging her maid, Aravis made her escape.

The children and the horses continue their journey until they approach Tashbaan. They agree to meet among the Tombs of the ancient kings on the edge of the desert beyond the city, in case they get separated.

The travellers enter the city but they haven't gone far before disaster strikes. They run into a grand procession on a state visit to the ruler of Tashbaan, the Tisroc. The people are fair-skinned like Shasta not like the dark-skinned men of the South; and, as they pass, one of them suddenly spots Shasta and seems to recognise him.

It is King Edmund who has mistaken Shasta for Prince Corin, son of the King of Archenland, who has been missing from the royal party for some hours.

Edmund takes Shasta to Queen Susan and a group of Narnians including Tumnus the faun. They treat Shasta royally and he is far too nervous to explain their mistake.

Anvard

Shasta overhears Edmund and Susan talking and learns that the King and Queen are facing trouble. Until now they have been treated as honoured guests, but the Tisroc's son, Prince Rabadash, wishes to marry Queen Susan and Edmund fears that if she refuses him (as she intends to do) they may become prisoners in Tashbaan.

Tumnus devises a scheme for their escape: Queen Susan is to invite Prince Rabadash to a banquet aboard the royal ship, the *Splendour Hyaline*. This will give the Narnians a chance to go back and forth to the ship, without arousing suspicion, and prepare for their departure. Then, as soon as night falls, they will sail away.

Leaving Shasta alone, the Narnians begin their preparations. But the boy is discovered by the *real* Prince Corin who tells Shasta how to find his way out of the city. Wishing each other luck, the boys part as friends with Corin telling Shasta to go to his father, King Lune, if he gets into any trouble.

Shasta manages his escape and reaches the Tombs, "great masses of mouldering stone shaped like gigantic beehives". There he waits for his friends, but they do not come and eventually the sun goes down.

The next day dawns, but still his friends do not arrive. Meanwhile, Aravis has been seen in the city by Lasara-leen, an old friend of hers who takes Aravis to her home. To her horror, Aravis learns that her father is in Tash-baan looking for her.

Lasaraleen is a silly girl, only interested in gossip and clothes, but Aravis finally convinces her friend to help her reach the Tombs undetected. Lasaraleen tells Aravis that there is a door out of the city in the Tisroc's garden.

A plan is made: a groom is to take the horses and wait outside Tashbaan and Aravis is to go to the Tisroc's palace disguised as Lasaraleen's slave-girl.

In the palace, the girls get lost and overhear a conversation between the ruler of Tashbaan, his son Prince Rabadash and Ahoshta Tarkaan, the old man Aravis was supposed to have married. Aravis learns that because Queen Susan has refused to marry Rabadash, the Prince is planning to invade first Anvard, the capital of Archenland, and then Narnia itself.

The Tisroc of Tashbaan

Aravis manages her escape from the palace and meets Shasta at the Tombs. The children decide to ride to Anvard to warn King Lune. Crossing the desert, they reach a narrow valley with rock walls on either side and, at last, enter Archenland. Then, looking back, they see Rabadash and his army on the march.

As the horses break into a gallop, they are once more pursued by the lion who snaps at the horses and scratches Aravis's back. Just in time, they find safety with an old Hermit who looks after Aravis and the horses and sends Shasta running north to King Lune.

He finds the King out hunting and warns him of Rabadash's planned attack. Shasta rides with the King

King Edmund leads the Narnians to war

towards Anvard, but the boy gets lost in a fog and is separated from the company. Shasta is joined by Aslan who tells the boy that he has been protecting him and spurring him along throughout his adventure.

The next day, Shasta – who has now found his way into Narnia – meets some of the Talking Beasts. A stag takes a message from the boy to King Edmund while Shasta is looked after by three dwarfs named Rogin, Duffle and Bricklethumb.

Later, Shasta meets King Edmund, Queen Lucy and Prince Corin as they march to war. The battle between Prince Rabadash and the army of Narnia at the gates of Anvard is watched by Aravis and the horses in a magic pool at the Hermit's house.

After the battle, which the Narnians win and in which Shasta is wounded, the boy learns that he is really Corin's brother, Prince Cor, who was kidnapped when he was a baby so that an old prophecy that he would one day save Archenland should not come true. Aslan reveals himself to Bree and Hwin and then to Aravis.

As the older of the two brothers, Cor becomes King of Archenland after King Lune and marries Aravis.

Rabadash

Following the departure of the four Pevensie children in 1015, a period of 1288 years pass before there is any more contact between our world and Narnia. During that time, Ram the Great succeeds Cor as King of Archenland and, in 1998, the Telemarines invade and conquer Narnia and Caspian I becomes King.

Two hundred and ninety-two years later, Prince Caspian, son of Caspian IX, is born, although the child's father is killed by Miraz (the brother of Caspian IX) who seizes the throne of Narnia. The events of the next thirteen years form part of the story told in…

Prince Caspian
(THE RETURN TO NARNIA)

It is 1941 and – a year after their first visit to Narnia – Peter, Edmund, Susan and Lucy Pevensie are sitting in a railway station waiting for a train to take them back to school.

Suddenly the children are pulled out of this world into Narnia. They find themselves on an island among an overgrown ruin and, after a while, realise that this was once the castle of Cair Paravel where they were Kings and Queens. Locating the treasure house, they find the gifts that Father Christmas had given them – except for one, Susan's horn, which is missing.

The children see two men row a boat down the river and then prepare to throw a bundle into the water. Realising that the bundle is alive, Susan fires an arrow from her Narnian bow and the men dive into the river and swim to safety.

They catch the boat and untie the bundle which turns out to be a dwarf named Trumpkin, who claims to be a messenger of King Caspian. So much seems to have happened since the children were in Narnia, Trumpkin has to give them a history lesson…

Prince Caspian, whose people were Telmarines, grew up with his uncle and aunt, King Miraz and Queen Prunaprismia. Miraz had murdered Caspian's father and had sent seven noble lords, who would have supported the young prince's claim to the throne, away to explore the Eastern Seas beyond the Lone Islands.

During his childhood, Caspian's nurse told him wonderful tales of Old Narnia, of animals that could talk and of the four Kings and Queens and Aslan the great Lion.

Doctor Cornelius

Not wanting his nephew to hear such stories, Miraz sent the prince's nurse away and arranged for him to be tutored by an old man named Doctor Cornelius. To Caspian's delight, Doctor Cornelius also knew the history of Old Narnia and, one night, the old man took the boy up on to the roof of the Great Tower of Miraz's castle to talk to him in secret.

Doctor Cornelius told Caspian something of what Narnia was like before it was invaded by the Telmarines: it was, said the Doctor, "the country of Aslan, the country of Walking Trees... of Fauns and Satyrs, of Dwarfs and Giants...of Talking Beasts..."

The Prince learned that his tutor was really a half-dwarf, and Doctor Cornelius asked Caspian to do everything he could to protect what was left of Old Narnia since, one day, he might become its king.

The Pevensie children discover the treasure house in Cair Paravel

Years passed and Caspian grew to realise what a cruel king his uncle had become. Then came a night when Doctor Cornelius told the boy that he was in danger and must leave the castle: the Queen had given birth to a son and there was now every chance that Miraz would try to kill Caspian just as he had killed his father.

Doctor Cornelius gave Prince Caspian the horn of Queen Susan, telling him: "Whoever blows it shall have strange help – no one can say how strange." Then the boy saddled his horse and rode off into the night.

The dwarfs and the badger look after Caspian

As Caspian galloped through the woods, he took a fall from his horse. He was found by two dwarfs, Nikabrik and Trumpkin, and a badger named Trufflehunter. Caspian told them his story and, after some argument, the badger and the dwarfs agreed to help him.

Caspian was taken to meet some of the other Old Narnians including Patterwig, Glenstorm and Reepicheep. Then, at the faun's Dancing Lawn, Caspian held a great council where it was agreed, on Doctor Cornelius's advice, that they should go to Aslan's How, "a very magical place, where there stood – and perhaps still stands – a very magical Stone…"

Prince Caspian and his followers set up their headquarters at Aslan's How, but Miraz found out where they were and made camp nearby. Various skirmishes took place and things seemed to be going against Caspian's army. Meeting round the Stone Table (on which Aslan had been killed), it was agreed that the time had come to sound Queen Susan's horn. When Caspian had done that, Trumpkin was sent to Cair Paravel to see if any help came…

When Trumpkin has finished his story, Peter, Susan, Edmund and Lucy tell the dwarf who they are, but he only believes them when he sees how skilled Edmund and Susan are with the sword and the bow.

They all set out in the boat rowing up the coast and then down Glasswater Creek so as to get as close as possible to Aslan's How. But there have been so many changes in Narnia over the years that, when they start to cross country, the children get lost. Lucy suddenly sees Aslan, but nobody else does and they ignore Lucy's advice and go in the opposite direction.

After a difficult journey, they find they are heading towards Miraz's troops, so they retrace their steps and camp for the night. Lucy wakes to see the trees beginning to dance with Aslan among them.

Aslan talks to Lucy and she then wakes the others who reluctantly agree to follow her. As they go, the others slowly begin to see Aslan. Peter, Susan and Edmund are reunited with the Lion and, having tossed Trumpkin into the air, Aslan makes friends with the dwarf.

Aslan sends Trumpkin and the boys ahead to Aslan's How, then he starts to roar and, as he does so, Narnia begins to awake. Aslan and the girls join in a wonderful romp with the creatures of the woodlands.

At Aslan's How new trouble is afoot: Prince Caspian, Doctor Cornelius and Trufflehunter are in conference with Nikabrik and two unpleasant characters. Because nothing seems to have happened as a result of Caspian blowing Queen Susan's horn, Nikabrik has another scheme: to call up the White Witch from the dead and seek her aid. When the prince and his advisers won't agree, the dwarf and his companions attack them.

Nikabrik and his evil companions attack Prince Caspian and friends

Peter, Edmund and Trumpkin burst into the room in time to see their friends fighting with Nikabrik, a Werwolf ("a horrible, grey, gaunt creature, half-man and half-wolf") and a Hag whose "nose and chin stuck out like a pair of nutcrackers". The fight is soon over and

the villains dead. Then Peter sends a challenge to King Miraz to meet him for a duel. It is received by Lord Glozelle and Lord Sopespian who, scheming to rule instead of Miraz, convince the King to accept Peter's call to combat.

The time for the duel arrives and, for a while, things go badly for Peter; but then the fight begins to go Peter's way and, at last, Miraz is brought to the ground. The Lords Glozelle and Sopespian join the fight and kill Miraz; the pitched battle breaks out between the Old Narnians and the Telmarines.

At last the enemy fly for their lives, but on reaching the river they find that the bridge is down and Aslan is coming with Susan, Lucy and all kinds of strange creatures awakened by the Lion. Also there, to Caspian's great joy, is the prince's old nurse who first told him tales of Narnia's past.

The Lords Glozelle and Sopespian

Aslan makes Caspian King of Narnia, and the young monarch knights Trumpkin, Trufflehunter and Reepicheep (who lost his tail in the battle but is given a new one by Aslan). Doctor Cornelius becomes King Caspian's Lord Chancellor and all the friends celebrate with a great feast.

The next day, everyone sees that a doorway of three pieces of wood has been put up. Aslan explains to the Telmarines where their people came from: how a shipload of pirates were stranded by a storm on an island in the South Seas of our world and how they had found their way through a cave into Narnia. Then Aslan offers the Telmarines the chance to go back. One by one they walk through the doorway and disappear.

The camp at Aslan's How

It is also time for the children to go and Aslan tells Peter and Susan that they are leaving Narnia for good. After changing out of their royal clothes, the Pevensies go through Aslan's door only to find themselves back on the railway station waiting for the train to school.

In Narnia it is three years since Caspian became King and, during that time, he has fought and defeated a band of giants on the northern frontier of Narnia. In England one year has passed since Peter, Susan, Edmund and Lucy returned from Aslan's world.

The children's parents and Susan are visiting America; Peter is studying for an examination with Professor Kirke and Edmund and Lucy are staying with their Uncle Harold and Aunt Alberta in Cambridge.

The worst thing about this arrangement is having to spend the holidays with their cousin, Eustace Scrubb. Eustace is spoilt and conceited and does his best to make their stay a miserable one.

In Lucy's bedroom, however, there is a wonderful picture of a sailing ship with a dragon's-head prow. Edmund and Lucy are convinced it is a Narnian ship and, one day, when Eustace is making fun of the others and their stories about Narnia, the ship in the picture begins to move. Then, magically, they are all pulled through the frame and fall into the sea.

They are rescued by the people on the ship – which

is called the *Dawn Treader* – among them King Caspian; Lord Drinian; and the valiant mouse Reepicheep.

Caspian tells Edmund and Lucy that he has made an oath to Aslan to search for the seven loyal lords who, many years before, were sent to explore the Eastern Seas. Reepicheep, however, wants to find a way to Aslan's country at the very eastern end of the world. Lucy and Edmund are delighted to be a part of this adventure, but Eustace is seasick and very unhappy.

Eventually they sight the Lone Islands, Doorn, Avra and Felimath, where Caspian, Reepicheep and the children go ashore. Almost immediately, they are captured by a gang of slave traders led by a man named Pug.

Everyone except the King is taken to Pug's slave ship where they are held prisoner. Caspian, however, is sold to a man who turns out to be one of the missing nobles, Lord Bern. He tells Caspian that the Islands are being badly ruled by a governor called Gumpas.

On Lord Bern's advice, Caspian visits the governor and pretends to have a fleet of ships waiting offshore. Then he throws Gumpas out, makes Lord Bern governor in his place, and rescues Edmund, Lucy and Eustace from the slave traders.

Three weeks later, they continue with their voyage and, after many days of difficult sailing they arrive at an inhospitable island.

Poor Eustace writes in his diary: "It would be bad enough even if one was with decent people instead of fiends in human form." The moment Eustace

Eustace and the dying dragon

gets ashore, he slips away on his own. He comes to a valley where he sees a monstrous creature with "a long lithe body that trailed on the ground". As Eustace watches, the dragon (for that is what it is) dies.

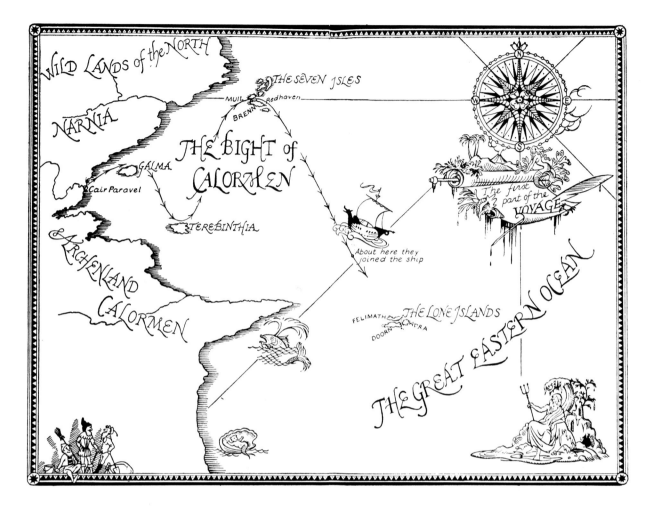

Caught in a rainstorm, Eustace takes shelter in the dragon's lair. Inside he finds a great hoard of treasure, puts a diamond-studded bracelet on his arm and falls asleep. When he awakes, Eustace finds, to his horror, that *he* has now turned into a dragon.

When the others see the Eustace-dragon, Caspian recognises the bracelet as the arm-ring which belonged to Octesian, one of the seven lords, but it takes them some time to realise who the dragon really is. Eustace is eventually rescued by Aslan who scratches away the scaly skin.

It is a very different Eustace who rejoins the party

when they finally sail away from Dragon Island.

After being attacked by a sea-serpent, they land on an island where they discover a pool that turns things to gold. At the bottom of the pool lies a golden statue of another of the seven lords, named Restimar, who must have been turned to gold while bathing.

The prospect of using the pool to produce great wealth leads to an argument between Caspian and Edmund that is only ended by the appearance of Aslan. Naming the place Deathwater Island, the Prince and his companions once more set sail.

On the next island they visit, Lucy becomes separated from the others and hears strange thumping noises and curious voices although no one is to be seen.

The invisible creatures threaten to kill the travellers unless Lucy goes into a house owned by a Magician and finds a book containing a spell.

The following day, Lucy enters the house and finds the book which contains a wonderful story that she forgets as soon as she has read it. There is no way of re-reading it since the pages of the book will not turn back. "It was about a cup and a sword and a tree and a green hill, I know that much. But I can't remember…"

At last Lucy locates the spell "to make hidden things visible" and says it. Immediately Aslan becomes visible to Lucy and he takes her to meet the Magician.

From the Magician, Coriakin, Lucy learns that the voices belonged to the Duffers who have been "uglified" into one-footed Monopods.

The *Dawn Treader* then sails to the Dark Island, a place of fears and night-mares. There they rescue an old man who is the Lord Rhoop and are guided out of the darkness by Aslan in the shape of an albatross.

The "uglified" Duffers. ("Uglify" is a word invented by Lewis Carroll in "Alice's Adventures in Wonderland".)

Caspian and the others land on an island where, in a great hall, they find three sleeping figures – the last of the lost lords, Revilian, Argoz and Mavramorn – sitting at a table spread with a magnificent banquet.

They meet Ramandu, who was once a star in the skies above Narnia, and his beautiful daughter. The three lords, says Ramandu, had quarrelled and touched a Knife of Stone that was lying on the table (the very knife used by the White Witch to kill Aslan). As a result, they now sleep, without dreaming.

Lord Rhoop is left to sleep with the other lords, in the care of Ramandu and his daughter.

They next sail through the Silver Sea and Reepicheep prepares to go to the very end of the world in search of Aslan's country. Caspian wants to go as well, but the children persuade him that his place is in Narnia.

Edmund, Lucy and Eustace set out in a boat with Reepicheep and, when they run aground, the mouse paddles away alone in a little coracle.

The children continue on foot and find a Lamb standing by a fire on which freshly-caught fish are cooking. When Lucy asks if they are heading for Aslan's country, the Lamb replies that, for them, the door into Aslan's country is from their own world. "There is a way into my country from all worlds," says the Lamb and he turns into Aslan.

Aslan tells Edmund and Lucy that they will not return to Narnia again and then, opening a door in the sky, he sends them back to Eustace's home in Cambridge.

On the homeward voyage to Narnia, Caspian marries Ramandu's daughter. In 2325, Prince Rilian is born; then, when the Prince is twenty, his mother is killed by a most evil creature. How that happened and what became of Rilian is told in . . .

Ramandu

(Opposite)
As the "Dawn Treader" approaches the Last Sea, the travellers encounter the Sea-People riding out on an underwater hunting expedition on sea-horses

It is just a few months after Eustace Scrubb visited Narnia, and he is back at his school, Experiment House, run by people who have "the idea that boys and girls should be allowed to do what they liked".

What a lot of older boys and girls like doing is bullying the younger pupils, and one of them who is bullied is Eustace's friend Jill Pole.

Finding Jill hiding behind the gym, Eustace tells her about Narnia and suggests they try to find their way there. Chased by bullies, they go through a door in the school wall and find themselves in another world.

They are on a very high cliff and, when Jill gets too near the edge, Eustace tries to pull her back only to lose his balance and fall. But Aslan appears and uses his powerful breath to blow Eustace to safety.

The Lion tells Jill that she and Eustace must find Narnia's Prince Rilian and gives her four signs which, if followed, will help them in their quest. First: Eustace will meet an old friend and must greet him at once. Second: they must journey to the ruined city of the ancient giants. Third: there they will find something written on stone and must do what it says. Fourth: they will know the lost prince because he will be the first person to ask them to do something in the name of Aslan.

Then the Lion uses his breath to send Jill to join Eustace in Narnia. She arrives as Eustace is watching an elderly king go aboard a ship in the harbour at Cair Paravel. Jill tells Eustace about the first of Aslan's signs, but he sees nobody that he recognises.

As the ship takes to the sea, the children meet an owl named Glimfeather who tells them the old king they have just seen is Caspian. Because Eustace had forgotten that "Narnian time flows differently from ours", he has missed the first sign and lost an opportunity of help.

Glimfeather takes Jill and Eustace, riding on his back, to a parliament of the King's Owls and there the children learn something of Prince Rilian's history...

Glimfeather carries Jill to the Parliament of Owls

One day the young prince had gone riding with his mother. The Queen decided to stop and rest and, as she slept, a great green serpent had come and bitten her. Almost at once the Queen had died of the poison.

Accompanied by his father's old friend, Lord Drinian, Rilian searched high and low to find and kill the serpent. Then, one day after they had met a beautiful woman dressed all in green, Prince Rilian had gone off alone and never returned...

The Black Knight and the mysterious Lady of the Green Kirtle. (Kirtle is an Old English word for a dress)

When Eustace and Jill tell the owls about the instructions given them by Aslan, the birds take them to Ettinsmoor where they meet Puddleglum the Marshwiggle who wears a high pointed hat "like a steeple" and has greeny-grey hair, webbed feet, and "a long thin face with rather sunken cheeks, a tightly shut mouth, a sharp nose and no beard".

Puddleglum agrees to take them north. Setting out across the wild waste lands they pass some old giants who throw stones at them. Then they meet a knight in black armour with the visor on his helmet closed who rides with a lady dressed in green.

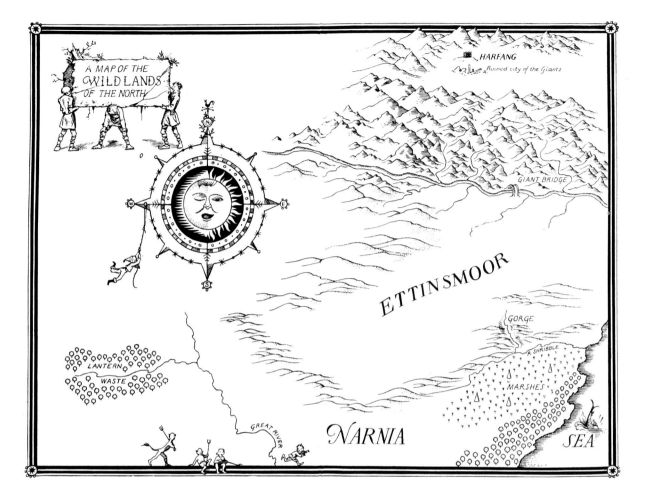

The knight is silent but the lady speaks to them. Although she says that she does not know the way to the Ruinous City, she suggests they go to the castle of Harfang, home of the Gentle Giants, where they may find help. The travellers are to tell the giants that she has sent them to Harfang for the giants' Autumn Feast.

Eustace, Jill and Puddleglum go on looking for the Ruinous City but get lost in bad weather. After wandering for some time in strange stone trenches, they see the castle of Harfang and decide to take the lady's advice.

They reach Harfang and find the giants very hospitable. In the castle, they come across a map from which they discover that when they had thought they were lost they were actually in the Ruinous City. Worse than that, the stone trenches where they had wandered for so long were really giant-sized letters carved to spell the words UNDER ME.

To the three friends' distress, they realise they have failed to recognise two of Aslan's signs. Then, to their even greater horror, they learn that they are going to be items on the menu at the giants' Autumn Feast.

The children and the Marsh-wiggle escape from Harfang but are pursued by the giants. They hide in a cave but it is so dark they lose their footing and slip and slide downwards for a long, long way.

When they reach the bottom they are confronted by the Warden of the Marches of Underland and his army of gnome-like Earthmen armed with pitchforks. The Earthmen place the strangers under guard and take them to the Queen of the Deep Realm.

The giants of Harfang

On the way they pass through an underground forest of mosses where strange dragonish creatures who have come from the land above now lie sleeping. In another cave they see Father Time who was once a king in Overland. Like the creatures in the forest, he sleeps till the end of the world.

Eustace, Jill and Puddleglum are taken on board a ship and rowed across a dark sea to a great city. The Earthmen take their prisoners to the castle but the Queen is away so the children and the Marsh-wiggle are brought before a young man who turns out to be the black knight they had seen escorting the beautiful lady in green.

Prince Rilian fights the green serpent

The knight tells the travellers his story: how the Queen of Underland had saved him from an evil enchantment that will only be broken when the Earthmen have dug through to the world above and the Queen makes him King of the Uplanders.

He also tells them that for one hour each night he changes into a terrible serpent and so must be tied to a silver chair. When that hour arrives he orders the children to tie him up but, instead of turning into a serpent, he claims to be free of his enchantment and perfectly sane. In desperation he begs to be untied.

The others hesitate until he calls on them to set him free "by the great Lion, by Aslan himself…". Then they recognise the fourth sign and, releasing the knight, find they have freed none other than Prince Rilian.

With one blow of his sword, Rilian destroys the silver chair that has held him prisoner for so long. But before they can escape, the Queen of Underland (who is also known as the Green Witch) returns to her castle. She lights a fire that gives off a drowsy fragrance and she then begins to play a mandolin.

The Witch's music weaves an enchantment over the prince and the others and they start wondering whether the things they think they remember about the Overland aren't just dreams and make-believe.

It is Puddleglum who keeps his wits and, stamping out the fire with his webbed feet, tells the Witch: "Suppose we *have* only dreamed, or made up, all those things…then all I can say is that…the made-up things seem a good deal more important than the real ones."

At this the Witch changes herself into a great green serpent just as she had done when she killed Rilian's mother. Helped by the children and the Marsh-wiggle, Prince Rilian fights the serpent and hacks off its head.

When they learn that the Witch is dead, the Earth-

(Opposite)
Eustace, Jill and Puddleglum meet the Earthmen of Underland

men are very happy and their pleasure is complete when a crack opens in Underland (which the gnomes call the Shallow Lands) and the Really Deep Land of Bism is revealed where it is so hot that precious metals and stones live and grow and may be eaten like fruit.

A gnome called Golg shows Prince Rilian, Edmund, Puddleglum and Jill the road to Overland and then hurries off to join his fellow Earthmen in the Land of Bism.

The four friends find their way to the earth's surface where they are dug out by dwarfs, moles, bears, badgers and other Narnian creatures.

Leaving Puddleglum to have his burnt foot nursed by the Talking Beasts, Edmund and Jill follow Prince Rilian to Cair Paravel and arrive in time to see him reunited with his father only moments before the old king dies.

Suddenly the great Lion appears and takes Jill and Eustace up on to the Mountain of Aslan. There, in a stream, lies the dead body of King Caspian. Then Eustace is ordered by Aslan to take a thorn and pierce the Lion's foot. Aslan's blood splashes into the stream and Caspian grows young again and comes back to life. In Narnia he is dead, but in Aslan's country he will live forever.

Eustace and Jill are sent back to their own world, briefly accompanied by

Narnians

Aslan and Caspian who give the headmistress and pupils of Experiment House a fright they will never forget!

Following the death of Caspian X, King Rilian rules Narnia well and the land was happy.

In 2534 there is trouble with outlaws in the north-western part of Narnia known as Lantern Waste. We know very little else about the 199 years of Narnian history between King Rilian and King Tirian, the last of the Kings of Narnia. His story is told in . . .

The Last Battle

It is the year 2555 in Narnia and living in Lantern Waste is Shift, "the cleverest, ugliest, most wrinkled ape you can imagine". Nearby lives a rather simple donkey called Puzzle who is always being tricked into doing things for the clever Shift.

One day by Caldron Pool, Shift sees something floating in the water that turns out to be a lion's skin. The ape dresses Puzzle in the skin and persuades him to pretend to be Aslan.

Three week's later, news of Aslan's return to Narnia reaches King Tirian and his companion Jewel the unicorn. But Roonwit the centaur, who studies the stars, warns Tirian that the only signs he has seen show a great evil threatening Narnia and that the stars say nothing about the coming of Aslan.

Their discussion is interrupted by the arrival of a wood nymph who tells the King that the Talking Trees in Lantern Waste are being cut down. Sending Roonwit to Cair Paravel to raise an army, Tirian and Jewel set out to discover the truth about the return of Aslan.

On the way they meet a water rat, taking logs downstream, who tells them that the tree-felling has been ordered by Aslan himself. Then the King and the unicorn come upon a gang of Calormenes cutting down trees. Two of the southerners are forcing Talking Horses to haul timber.

Poggin

Tirian and Jewel kill the Calormenes and are at once attacked by the rest of the men. The King escapes on Jewel's back, but both feel guilty about murdering two unarmed men, especially if they were carrying out the orders of Aslan.

So they return, give themselves up and ask to be taken to Aslan. The Calormenes lead Tirian and Jewel to the top of a hill where Shift sits outside a small stable.

The ape claims to be telling the Narnian animals Aslan's orders: horses, donkeys and bulls are to be sent south to work for the ruler of Calormen, the Tisroc, while the dwarfs and moles will be needed to dig in the Tisroc's mines.

Griffle

The animals are confused and one little lamb asks how Aslan can be a friend of the Tisroc when the Calormenes serve the vulture-headed god, Tash. Shift replies that Tash and Aslan are one and the same and when Tirian and Jewel protest at this, the unicorn is led away and the King tied to a tree to await punishment.

Shift gives orders

As night falls, a group of faithful Talking Beasts set Tirian free. Then, when it is completely dark, he returns to Stable Hill. By the light of a great bonfire, he sees Shift bring Aslan out of the stable and show him to the Narnians. Everyone believes that Puzzle is really the great Lion, except for Tirian who calls to the real Aslan and to the Friends of Narnia, for help.

Tirian has a kind of dream in

which he sees seven curiously-dressed people sitting round a table. Though he does not know it, he is looking at Professor Digory Kirke, Polly Plummer, Peter, Edmund and Lucy Pevensie, Jill Pole and Eustace Scrubb. Then the dream fades and, almost at once, Jill and Eustace appear in Narnia.

Tash carries off Rishda Tarkaan

The children explain to the King that the seven friends of Narnia had met because Digory had a feeling that their help was needed. After they saw Tirian they had made various plans: Peter and Edmund had been sent to London, to Digory's old house, to dig up the Magic Rings that were buried in the garden so they could be used by Eustace and Jill, the only two of the friends who could still return to Narnia.

Jill and Eustace were going back to school by train, accompanied by Polly, Digory, Lucy and, coincidentally, the Pevensies' parents. On the way they were to meet Peter and Edmund so that the Rings could be handed over. But as the train had approached the station where Peter and Edmund were waiting, Jill and Eustace had suddenly found themselves in Narnia.

When they have told their story, Tirian takes the children to where they can disguise themselves with Calormene armour. Then they set out for the stable where they find Jewel and discover Puzzle in his lion skin.

A short time later, they meet and rescue a party of dwarfs being taken by Calormen guards to the Tisroc's mine. Tirian explains how Shift had deceived the Narnians, but the dwarfs refuse to believe the King's story or that there is any Aslan whatsoever. As they go on, one of the dwarfs, called Poggin, follows Tirian and offers his help.

Poggin gives the King some important news: because Shift has begun to drink heavily, the plot is now being

masterminded by the Calormen captain, Rishda Tarkaan, and by a talking cat named Ginger.

As they are talking they suddenly see a fearful creature going northward through the woods and realise it is Tash. Shortly afterwards they learn from Far-sight the Eagle the news that Cair Paravel has been captured by Calormenes and that Roonwit the centaur has been killed.

Far-sight the eagle

The King and his friends return to Stable Hill, planning to show the disguised Puzzle to the Narnians. But when they get there they hear Shift warning everyone that a donkey is wandering in the woods pretending to be Aslan.

Ginger and Shift

The rebellious dwarfs begin to doubt if there is anything in the stable, but Shift calls for a volunteer to go in and meet Tashlan (as they are now referring to him).

Ginger, who is obviously part of the scheme, steps forward and walks calmly through the door. A few seconds later, he comes hurtling out again, no longer able to speak.

Tirian challenges the enemies of Narnia to fight and the last great battle begins. The King throws Shift into the stable and "a blinding greenish-blue light" shines out, the earth shakes and there is a strange noise – "a clucking and screaming" like the hoarse voice of some monstrous bird.

As the fight goes on, the Calormenes throw a group of dwarfs into the stable and Jill and Eustace follow. Then Tirian goes through the door dragging Rishda Tarkaan with him.

Inside, Tirian finds he is outside. There is no stable – only a door – and it's not night but day. Facing him are Narnia's friends from our world (only Susan is not among them, being no longer a friend of Narnia). But he also sees Tash who (having already gobbled up the ape) seizes Rishda and carries him off.

Digory, Polly, Peter, Edmund, Lucy, Jill and Eustace explain to Tirian that they, and Mr and Mrs Pevensie, have all been involved in a railway accident and so are dead in their world.

Tirian and the others try to help the dwarfs who continue to believe they are inside a dark, smelly stable. Even when Aslan arrives they still refuse to see what everyone else can see.

"Now it is time!" says Aslan. "TIME!" And the door flies open.

Through the doorway they see Narnia in darkness. Father Time awakes and sounds a horn. Then dragons and lizards come down from the mountains and all the creatures in the land stream towards the door and Aslan.

Some look at the Lion and are so afraid they fall away into the shadows; others look at him with love and go through the door – among them Jewel, Roonwit, Farsight and Poggin. Then the final night falls and the seas engulf Narnia. On Aslan's order the High King Peter shuts and locks the door.

"Come further in! Come further up!" Aslan calls to everyone and they all follow where he leads until they come to Aslan's country and a garden on a hill where they are met by Reepicheep the mouse and all their old friends: Puddleglum; Trufflehunter; Trumpkin; Glimfeather; King Rilian; Fledge the flying horse; King Frank and Queen Helen; Cor, Aravis and Corin; King Caspian and Tumnus the faun.

Inside the garden they find a whole other world with Aslan waiting for them. The great lion pardons Puzzle the donkey and welcomes the others: "The dream has ended," he tells them, "this is the morning…"

Puzzle

The Last Battle is the final book of The Chronicles of Narnia. When Jack Lewis was asked why he had stopped writing about Narnia, he said: "There are only two times at which you can stop a thing: one is before everyone is tired of it, the other is after."

Some grown-ups complained that parts of the books were too frightening for children. "But," Jack said, "the real children like it, and I am astonished how some very young ones seem to understand it. I think it frightens some adults but few children."

When *The Last Battle* was published in 1956, it won the Carnegie Medal for the best children's book of the year. And for many readers, it is the best of all the stories. Although, perhaps, as one true friend of Narnia has remarked: "Our favourite book about Narnia is usually the one we happen to be reading right now..."

Night falls on Narnia

BETWEEN THE LAMP-POST AND THE GREAT CASTLE

When Mr Tumnus tells Lucy, in *The Lion, the Witch and the Wardrobe*, that she is in Narnia, she says: "Narnia? What's that?" To which the faun replies: "This is the land of Narnia where we are now; all that lies between the lamp-post and the great castle at Cair Paravel on the eastern sea..."

As we read *The Lion, The Witch and the Wardrobe* and the other six Chronicles, we discover more and more about the Land of Narnia and the countries around it. You can use Pauline Baynes's maps in *Prince Caspian, The Horse and His Boy, The Voyage of the "Dawn Treader"* and *The Silver Chair* (and in this book on pages 46, 56, 62 and 77) to find the places mentioned in the stories.

Remember, however, that it is impossible to be totally accurate about the geography of Narnia since the books cover a period of 2555 years and, during that time, many changes take place: woods and forests grow up, rivers change directions, new cities are built while old ones fall into ruins and whole nations, such as Calormen, become established where once there was nothing.

Many of the places, like Lantern Waste and Aslan's How, are magical and that, of course, is because Narnia is part of Another World.

Digory's Uncle Andrew says that a really Other World is "another Nature – another universe – somewhere you would never reach even if you travelled through the space of this universe for ever and ever – a world that could be reached only by Magic…"

What Digory and Polly discover, however is not *one* magic world but several. To begin with there is the Wood between the Worlds, which they reach using Magic Rings made out of dust from the lost city of Atlantis. "I don't believe," says Digory, "this is a world at all. I think it's just a sort of in-between world…a place that isn't in any of the worlds, but once you've found that place you can get into them all."

It is through two of the pools in this Wood that Polly and Digory visit first Charn and then the empty world that becomes Narnia. Although they never try any of the other pools, Digory believes there was probably Another World at the bottom of each of them. And years afterwards when he has become a professor, he tells later explorers of Narnia that "nothing is more probable" than that there are Other Worlds all over the place, just round the corner…

None of the other children who find themselves in Narnia go by way of the Wood between the Worlds; they get in through what Aslan refers to as "chinks and chasms" between Earth and Narnia.

One of those "chinks" is the wardrobe, another is the painting of the "Dawn Treader", while Jill and Eustace enter Narnia through a door in the school wall.

Eustace, Lucy and Edmund fall into the picture of the "Dawn Treader"

If you read the books carefully, you will find there are doors and gates (some magical and some ordinary) in every one of The Chronicles of Narnia. You may also be able to think of some other children's books which have magical doors in them like *Alice's Adventures in Wonderland, Mary Poppins Opens the Door* and *Tom's Midnight Garden*.

Regardless of *how* the children get into Narnia they all find a world that is quite different from their own.

King Tirian and King Peter inside the magical stable door

Narnia, for example, has its own stars such as Spearhead, Alambil and Tarva, and among its constellations are the Hammer, Leopard and Ship. The stars themselves are very unusual because when they grow old they go to live in human form on one of the islands of the Eastern Sea like Coriakin and Ramandu.

"In our world," Eustace tells Ramandu, "a star is a huge ball of flaming gas." To which the old man replies: "Even in your world, my son, that is not what a star is but only what it is made of."

Narnian stars, of course, were magical from the moment of their creation when, in answer to the song of the Lion, they began singing in "cold, tingling, silvery voices". Perhaps when Jack was writing this he remembered that, in medieval times, people in our world believed that the planets made a kind of music that they called the Music of Spheres.

You can read the full story of the creation of Narnia in *The Magician's Nephew* and you will see that it is a little like the creation stories told in the Bible and other old books. This story tells how people from Earth witness the making of a *new* world, when the great lion, Aslan, prowls through the darkness singing everything to life.

They watch as the earth of 'fresh, hot and vivid' colours grows grass, trees and wild flowers along the banks of a broad, swift river "flowing eastwards towards the sun".

The most surprising thing about Narnia is that it is flat. According to Reepicheep it is "like a great round table and the waters of all the oceans endlessly pouring over the edge". When the Lord Drinian asks the mouse what would be found at the bottom if a ship sailed off the edge, Reepicheep suggests that it might be the way to Aslan's Country, "or perhaps there isn't any bottom. Perhaps it goes down for ever and ever..."

Although Caspian's world isn't round like ours, it does have some things in common with this world such as cold northern lands and hot desert countries further south.

When Jack had completed *Prince Caspian*, he provided a rough sketch of Narnia to help Pauline Baynes in drawing the map for the book. Although Jack only showed places mentioned in his first two books, he did mark one place with an X, saying, "A future story will require marshes here. We needn't mark them now but must not put in anything inconsistent with them".

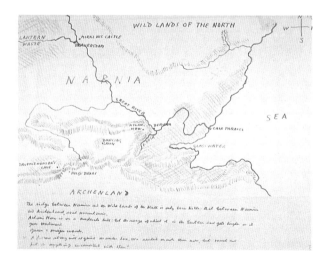

Jack's first map of Narnia drawn for Pauline Baynes

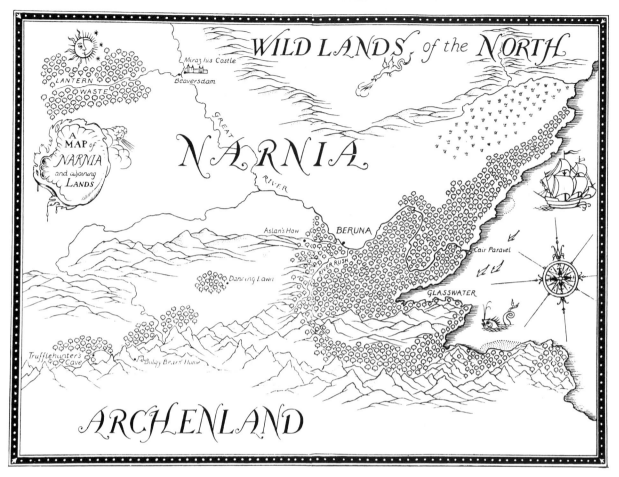

Actually, Pauline Baynes *did* draw the marshes on the map, but then they were not referred to until *The Silver Chair*, four books later. As more stories appeared, the artist provided additional maps, and eventually put together a full map of Narnia and the lands and islands round it – with the exception of the land of Telmar beyond the Western Mountains.

When you look at the country as a whole, you see that while Narnia is a beautiful land of woods and forest glades, crashing waterfalls and sparkling streams, the lands to the north and south are very different.

In the north lie the Wild Lands where you will find the ruined city of the giants and the castle of Harfang.

Maybe part of the inspiration for those lands came from Jack's fondness for the Norse sagas. Looking back, many years later, he remembered how as a boy he had loved these old legends with their stark landscapes in "the endless twilight of northern summer".

To the south of Narnia lies Archenland and, across another range of mountains, the desert and the country of Calormen where the mighty city of Tashbaan stands on an island in the middle of a great river.

The city of Tashbaan was influenced by Jack's childhood reading of "The Arabian Nights"

Apart from going to France to fight in the First World War and, towards the end of his life, taking a holiday in Greece, Jack never left the British Isles. And it is the countryside of Ireland and England that seems to have helped Jack create the Land of Narnia with its snow-capped mountains, heather-covered moors, dark pine woods, sunlit glades of oaks and beech trees, orchards white with cherry blossom and lazily winding rivers. It is because Jack describes the places in his stories so well that Narnia seems as real to us as it does.

Narnia also seems so real because the books are full of unforgettable accounts of food and drink which are like – but so much better than – the things we eat and drink.

In *The Lion, the Witch and the Wardrobe*, Mr Tumnus serves Lucy tea with boiled eggs, sardines, buttered toast and honey and sugar-topped cakes. A little later, Mr and Mrs Beaver give the children a wonderful supper of fried trout and new potatoes followed by a "gloriously sticky marmalade roll". What Jack doesn't explain is how they managed to find so much fresh food when there had been nothing but winter in Narnia for a hundred years – but perhaps all that ice and snow provided the Narnians with a kind of natural deep-freeze!

Lucy has tea with Mr Tumnus

Jack loved good food which is probably why his descriptions of feasts, like the one in *Prince Caspian*, are delightfully mouthwatering: "Sides of roasted meat that filled the grove with a delicious smell, and wheaten cakes and oaten cakes, honey and many-coloured sugars and cream thick as porridge and as smooth as still water, peaches, nectarines, pomegranates, pears, grapes, strawberries, raspberries – pyramids and cataracts of fruit. Then, in great wooden cups and bowls and mazers, wreathed with ivy, came the wines; dark, thick ones like red jellies liquefied, and yellow wines and green wines and yellow-green and greenish yellow…"

Of one particular food, of course, one has to be very careful: the White Witch's deadly Turkish Delight…

There are in Narnia many quite fantastical things, such as the lamp-post; money and toffee trees that accidentally grow there; and lots of very mysterious places around – and even *under* – the land itself.

One of the strangest places in Narnia must be Underland, beneath the Wild Lands of the north: a place of underground forests, rivers and cities. And a thousand fathoms below Underland is the Really Deep Land of Bism where there is a river of fire and "fields and groves of an unbearable, hot brilliance".

There are equally wonderful, curious and dangerous places among the islands visited by Caspian and the crew of the *Dawn Treader*: islands full of strange enchantments and frightening dreams and inhabited by dragons, one-footed dwarfs and living stars.

Jill, Eustace and Puddleglum travel through Underland, a world partly inspired by "A Journey to the Centre of the Earth" and "King Solomon's Mines"

And, beyond all these islands, in the far east, is a way into Aslan's Country. There are no maps of Aslan's Country (of which Narnia is just a reflection) but the characters in *The Last Battle* enter it through the gates of the walled garden on the green hill beyond the great waterfall. It was there, over two thousand years before, that Digory came to fetch the apple needed by Aslan to protect Narnia from the Witch Jadis. And it is there that all Narnia's true friends finally meet together.

As they approach the great golden gates, they wonder: "Dare we? Is it right? Can it be meant for *us*?" And then there is the sound of "a great horn, wonderfully loud and sweet", coming from somewhere inside that walled garden and the gates swing open...

The "Dawn Treader" approaches Dragon Island

Inside, they find not just a garden but a whole world, the *real* Narnia, and, far away, beyond the islands, they see the *real* England, of which the England they knew was also just a reflection.

Jack quite often wrote about gardens, and one reason for this may have been something which happened during his childhood in Ireland. One day, his brother Warnie brought into the nursery a miniature garden which he had made using the lid of an old biscuit tin covered with moss and twigs and flowers.

Long afterwards, Jack wrote: "That was the first beauty I ever knew. It made me aware of nature as something cool, dewy, fresh, exuberant...As long as I live, my imagination of Paradise will retain something of my brother's toy garden."

Perhaps if it hadn't been for Warnie's biscuit-tin garden, Jack might not have created all those beautiful and mysterious places that lie between, and beyond, the lamp-post and the castle at Cair Paravel.

The Castle of Cair Paravel

SOME QUEER SPECIMENS

If you create your own world you can not only decide what it will look like but what kind of beings will live there: you can have hobbits, jumblies, jabberwocks, oompa-loompas, pushmi-pullyus or toads that drive motor cars.

In the Land of Narnia we find an extraordinary collection of creatures – there are domestic animals, wild animals and imaginary animals all living alongside each other, together with witches, dwarfs, gods, men and monsters. No wonder Eustace remarks, at one point, that there seem to be "some queer specimens" among the inhabitants of Narnia.

The first animals to enter Narnia are very much like the animals in our world. The earth swells into lots of humps of different sizes which burst to reveal all kinds of birds, beasts and insects. Narnia is filled with "cawing, cooing, crowing, braying, neighing, baying, barking, lowing, bleating and trumpeting".

From these animals, Aslan chooses some to be Talking Beasts and breathes on them "a long warm breath". The Lion then puts them in charge of the Dumb Beasts he has not chosen. As well as receiving the power of speech, another change comes over these creatures: the smaller ones, like rabbits and moles, grow while very big ones, such as elephants, grow a little smaller.

Among the talking beasts are birds and animals similar to those found in the British countryside: squirrels, mice, foxes, badgers, hedgehogs, deer, robins, owls and jackdaws; as well as the kind we think of as pets or farm animals such as cats and dogs, horses, donkeys and cattle.

From when he was a boy until the end of his life, Jack Lewis kept pets and loved animals – even those most of us try to get rid of. "I love real mice," Jack told an American girl who sent him a drawing of Reepicheep. "There are lots in my rooms in college but I have never set a trap. When I sit up late working, they poke their heads out from behind the curtains just as if they were saying, 'Hi! Time for *you* to go to bed. We want to come out and play!'"

There are also many *wild* animals mentioned in The Chronicles of Narnia: bears, elephants, wart hogs, tapirs, elks, leopards, panthers and lions. There is even a reference to a pelican and if you look carefully at one of Pauline Baynes's pictures you will find giraffes, camels, zebra and a pair of ostriches.

Some of the wild animals – such as Mr and Mrs Beaver and the Bulgy Bears – are good and loyal to Aslan; but others are unpleasant, wicked creatures like Shift the ape who does so much harm to Narnia.

One of the most terrifying of these wild Narnians is the great wolf Maugrim who serves the White Witch. In American copies of *The Lion, the Witch and the Wardrobe* he is called Fenris Ulf, a name which Jack borrowed from a character in one of the Norse myths. The Fenris-Wolf was a huge beast who was feared by everyone until he was eventually tied up with a chain, made by dwarfs out of invisible things that never existed, like the roots of a mountain, the beard of a woman, the breath of a fish and the noise of a moving cat.

Edmund nervously approaches Maugrim (or Fenris-Ulf)

Eustace Scrubb after being turned into a dragon

Jack included a number of other mythological and legendary creatures in his books: there is a sea-serpent, a kraken and a phoenix as well as dragons, unicorns, mermaids, gnomes, giants and dwarfs, or "Sons of Earth" as Aslan calls them.

Both the giants and the dwarfs in Narnia are a mixed bunch: while some are good characters, quite a few of them side with Aslan's enemies.

Like the dwarfs in many old legends, those in Narnia are mostly miners and goldsmiths. They are all (despite their smallness) fiercely independent and (except for those in *The Magician's Nephew*) very suspicious of Aslan and his supporters. Among the worst are the White Witch's dwarf in *The Lion*, the treacherous Nikabrik in *Prince Caspian* and the stubborn Griffle and his stupid companions in *The Last Battle*. But there are also the good dwarfs Trumpkin (who eventually becomes King Caspian's regent) and brave little Poggin who joins Tirian in his fight against the Calormenes.

Narnian giants are all rather slow-witted; but while some like Rumblebuffin and Wimbleweather are courageous and kind-hearted, others are extremely unpleasant – as Jill, Eustace and Puddleglum discover to their cost when they visit the castle of Harfang.

There are two characters with magical powers who are still known in our world – Father Time, who sleeps in Underland, in a cave "about the shape and size of a cathedral"; and Father Christmas, "a huge man in a bright red robe (bright as holly berries)" and a great white beard that falls "like a foamy waterfall over his chest".

Giant Wimbleweather and friends

A river god

The majority of the strange beings in Narnia have their origins in the myths of ancient Greece and Rome. From these stories, Jack took the idea of river-gods and water-nymphs, called Naiads, who live in rivers, springs, lakes and wells. There are also woodland nymphs known as Dryads and Hamadryads, who are the spirits of the trees and who die when their tree is cut down.

The mythological characters which live in Narnia are much pleasanter than those written about in the stories of our world. For example, in Narnia, the centaurs (who are half-horse and half-man) are a brave, noble people whereas, in the Greek legends, they are often drunk and violent. One exception was a centaur named Chiron, who taught two of the Greek heroes, Achilles and Jason, and who was wise and gentle and skilled in medicine and archery. Perhaps it was Chiron who inspired Roonwit, the wise astronomer centaur in *The Last Battle*.

A wood nymph

King Tirian, Jewel and Roonwit the centaur

84

Like centaurs, quite a few mythical creatures are made up of parts from two or more ordinary animals, such as Pegasus the winged horse who obviously suggested the idea for Fledge, the cab-horse, who grew a pair of wings "larger than eagles', larger than swans', larger than angels' wings in church windows" with chestnut and copper-coloured feathers.

Bacchus, the Roman god of drink and celebration

From the Roman myths, Jack borrowed the gods of wine and merry-making, Bacchus and Silenus, and their fauns and satyrs who – like the god Pan – are half-goat and half-man. You may remember that among the books owned by the faun, Mr Tumnus, are *The Life and Letters of Silenus* and, a rather curious book for a mythical character to read, *Is Man a Myth?*

Pegasus

In Narnia, man is certainly not a myth. People have been here right from the beginning: the first King and Queen are a "Son of Adam" and a "Daughter of Eve" from our world. It is their descendents who, many years later, settled to the south of Narnia, in Archenland.

Then things start to go wrong when a gang of outlaws move further south, across the desert, and begin the kingdom of Calormen and, later, go west to Telmar.

And it is in Telmar that a ship-load of pirates finds its way into Narnia. The story of what happens when the Telmarines invade Narnia and how they are eventually taken back into our world is told in *Prince Caspian*.

Some of the most interesting characters in Narnia are those which are Jack's own creations like the Duffers whom Lucy meets on the Island of Voices during the voyage of the *Dawn Treader*. The Duffers, who were once ordinary dwarfs, are so disobedient that Coriakin the Magician "uglifies" them into one-legged Monopods. Then, because they cannot bear to look at one another, they use a spell in the Magician's magic book to make themselves invisible.

The Monopods, who sleep with their single enormous feet in the air above them so they look like mushrooms, are such silly creatures they plant boiled potatoes in order not to have to cook them when they dig them up! They finally become visible again and, when Lucy tells them that they look nice, they grow happy once more and call themselves Moneypuds, Pomonods, Poddymons and, eventually, Dufflepuds.

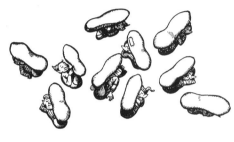

The Dufflepuds

Jack sent Pauline Baynes a sketch of the Dufflepuds to help with her illustration, and it seems likely that he got his idea for what they might look like from an ancient map of the world in Hereford Cathedral.

On the same voyage Lucy also meets the Sea-People of the Last Sea, who have dark purple hair and bodies "the colour of old ivory". Riding sea-horses, they go hunting with specially-trained fish that sit on their wrists, like hunters in our world used to do with falcons.

But perhaps Jack's most imaginative creation is the Marsh-wiggle, Puddleglum, who is a frog-like man with a somewhat gloomy personality that is rather like the character of Eeyore the donkey in A. A. Milne's *Winnie-the-Pooh* stories: "Good morning," Puddleglum says to Jill and Eustace, "though when I say *good* I don't mean it won't probably turn to rain or it might be snow, or fog or thunder..."

Puddleglum's character, it has been said, was based on that of Jack's elderly gardener, Fred Paxford, who was "an inwardly optimist, outwardly pessimistic, dear, frustrating, shrewd countryman of immense integrity". The name "Puddleglum" itself was inspired by a phrase Jack had come across in a sixteenth-century translation of a Latin poem entitled *Hippolytus*.

This picture of a thirteenth-century map of the world known as the Mappa Mundi, inspired Jack's delightful creatures, the Dufflepuds

Living in a wigwam and smoking tobacco mixed with mud, Puddleglum proved something of a puzzle to the illustrator, Pauline Baynes. This was the only occasion when she asked the author's advice. "Draw him however you like," Jack told her, so she drew him as a tall, thin creature with webbed feet, straggly hair and a rather solemn expression.

Puddleglum fishing in the marshes of Ettinsmoor

There are also in Narnia beings who are neither men, beasts nor mythological creatures. They have great powers and play an important role in the history of Narnia.

Two of them are witches: the Green Witch who is the Queen of Underland and who can turn herself into a great, green serpent. And older, and far more terrible, the White Witch who was once Queen Jadis of Charn.

While the Green Witch is served by the Earthmen, who are really kindly gnomes who work for her out of fear, the White Witch commands a terrible army of the most horrible creatures you can imagine. Among her company are giant bats and vultures and a host of monsters, ghosts, demons and evil spirits from English and Irish folk-lore and various myths from around the world. Their names alone are frightening: Ogres, Minotaurs, Cruels, Hags, Incubuses, Wraithes, Horrors, Efreets, Orknies, Wooses, Ettins, Ghouls, Spectres, Boggles, Werewolves and the people of the Toadstools.

You may notice from the way the White Witch is described when Edmund first meets her in *The Lion, the Witch and the Wardrobe* that she resembles a similarly wicked lady in Hans Christian Anderson's story *The Snow Queen*. But in her earlier form, as ruler of Charn, she is even more fearsome and dangerous and can destroy an entire world with the use of just one word.

Apart from these villainesses, there are two other powerful forces in the Land of Narnia. One is Tash, the hideous god of the Calormenes. A grey cloud of smoke in the shape of a creature with four arms, a beak and "long, pointed, bird-like claws instead of nails", Tash moves through Narnia withering the grass as he goes.

Tash is no figment of the imagination; although he is ugly and evil, he is also real. He is even allowed beyond the stable door into Aslan's Country in order to claim the treacherous Rishda, who has done terrible things in the name of Tash but who does not really believe in him.

But mightier than Tash is Aslan, the Son of the Emperor-beyond-the-Sea, the creator and King of Narnia. His name (which, according to Jack, should be pronounced *Ass-lan*) is the Turkish word for "lion" and was discovered by Jack in a copy of *The Arabian Nights*.

Aslan is strong and powerful, yet good and kind; he can be angry and terrible, gentle and loving. Jack said that Aslan was "the Lion of Judah", which is a name given to someone in the Bible and which Jack used because, as you will read in a moment, he wrote The Chronicles of Narnia to contain a "hidden story".

“I'm so thankful that you realized the 'hidden story' in the Narnian books,” Jack wrote to a young reader. “It is odd, children nearly *always* do, grown-ups hardly ever.”

What did Jack mean by the “hidden story”? He was telling us that there is something more to The Chronicles of Narnia than just exciting and entertaining adventures. They are stories with a *meaning*.

You may have come across other stories with a meaning such as the fables of Aesop. When we read the fable of *The Tortoise and the Hare* we can see it as just a funny story about how a very slow tortoise has a race with a fast-running hare and yet still manages to win; or we can see it as a story that shows how, sometimes, it is the most unexpected person who is successful.

Then there are other stories that have very special meanings, like the parables told by Jesus or John Bunyan's famous book *The Pilgrim's Progress*, which tells how a man called Christian sets out on a long and difficult journey. The journey represents Christian's life and the people he meets as he travels have unusual names – such as Faithful, Hopeful, Ignorance and Talkative – that tell us something about their character.

C. S. Lewis

Stories like this are called allegories, and one of Jack's first books, *The Pilgrim's Regress*, was closely modelled on Bunyan's story. The hero, named John, meets all kinds of strange people including the Clevers and the Cruels and visits, among other places, the Cities of Thrill and Claptrap.

The Chronicles of Narnia are not allegories and everyone and everything in them is not meant to represent something else. "A strict allegory," Jack told his god-daughter, Lucy, "is like a puzzle with a solution." His stories were meant to be more like "a flower whose smell reminds you of something you can't quite place". And, as some people read those stories, they do discover characters and situations that remind them of another very well known story...

C. S. LEWIS
The Pilgrim's Regress

Jack wrote his children's books in this way because "sometimes fairy stories may say best what's to be said", and he wanted to tell young readers some of the things he believed as a Christian in a way they would still enjoy reading about.

Remembering his own childhood and the way in which he had been taught about religion, he asked: "Why did one find it so hard to feel as one was told one ought to feel about God or about the sufferings of Christ? I thought the chief reason was that one was taught one ought to. The whole subject was associated with lowered voices; almost as if it was something medical." As a child Jack felt that trying to understand religion was like the hero of a fairy tale trying to sneak past dragons guarding a castle door.

Which is why Jack decided to take Christian ideas, get rid of what he called "their stained glass and Sunday School associations" and put them into a story set in an imaginary world. "Could one not thus steal past those watchful dragons? I thought one could ..."

What enabled him to do so was the arrival in his imagination of Aslan. And, having found his way into the first story, Aslan "pulled the six other Narnian stories in after him".

"It's a funny thing," Jack wrote two days before he died, "that all the children who have written to me see at once who Aslan is, and grown-ups *never* do!"

So, who *is* Aslan? In the last chapter of *The Voyage of the "Dawn Treader"*, Lucy, Edmund and Eustace travel to the Very End of the World where they meet a lamb who suddenly changes into the lion, Aslan. As he talks to the children, Aslan reveals that he is not just in Narnia but in our world as well. "But there," he says, "I have another name. You must learn to know me by that name. This is the very reason why you were brought into Narnia, that by knowing me here for a little, you may know me better there ..."

When a young girl from America wrote to Jack to ask what name Aslan used in our world, he replied:
As to Aslan's other name, well, I want you to guess. Has there ever been anyone in *this* world who
(1) Arrived at the same time as Father Christmas?
(2) Said he was the Son of the Great Emperor?
(3) Gave himself up for someone else's fault to be jeered at and killed by wicked people? (4) Came to life again?
(5) Is sometimes spoken of as a lamb? Don't you really know His name in this world? Think it over and let me know your answer!

That's one of the very few clues that Jack ever gave his readers about the meaning of the "hidden story" in his books, and it would be quite wrong for this book to try and explain things that he himself never explained.

Not everyone sees and understands the meaning behind The Chronicles of Narnia, but that doesn't matter. Narnia's illustrator, Pauline Baynes, only began to see it many years after she had done the pictures. It is interesting that Jack never once asked her if she understood what his stories were about – but perhaps he felt, looking at her pictures, that she understood without knowing it. After all, he once said that he wanted his stories to give people "a picture" rather than "a map".

When you next read The Chronicles of Narnia you may begin to see that picture and – if you haven't already done so – understand something of the "hidden story" behind the creation of Narnia, the betrayal and death of Aslan and the last days before Narnia comes to an end. If you do, then you will have seen beyond the Deep Magic that C. S. Lewis put into his books to a Deeper Magic from before the dawn of time.

THE STORY WHICH GOES ON FOREVER

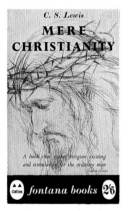

"For us," C. S. Lewis wrote in the final chapter of the *The Last Battle*, "this is the end of all the stories, and we can mostly truly say that they all lived happily ever after ...". But what happened to the creator of Narnia? Did he live happily ever after?

By the time *The Last Battle* was published, Jack Lewis was internationally famous, not just as a writer for children but also for his religious writings. He was rather surprised when books such as *Miracles* and *Mere Christianity* became best-sellers and people from all over the world started writing to him to ask for his help and advice.

Jack eventually decided to write an autobiography, telling the story of his life from his childhood in Ireland until the time when he became a Christian. He called the book *Surprised by Joy*, which was his way of describing the deep happiness that he had felt from time to time during his life.

It was quite a coincidence that in 1952 he found a different kind of joy when he met and grew to like an American writer, Joy Davidman, who was visiting England. The following year she came to live in London with her two sons, Douglas and David, and she often visited Jack and his brother Warnie (neither of whom had married) in their house in Oxford called The Kilns.

In 1947 Jack appeared on the cover of the famous American magazine "Time"

Eight-year-old Douglas had read the first four tales of Narnia and he was a little disappointed on first meeting C. S. Lewis. "Here was a man," he remembers thinking, "who was on speaking terms with King Peter, with the Great Lion, Aslan himself. Here was the man who had been to Narnia; surely he should at least wear silver chainmail and be girt about with a jewel-encrusted sword-belt."

The brothers Cor and Corin with King Lune in "The Horse and His Boy", which Jack dedicated to the brothers David and Douglas.

The very ordinary-looking Jack Lewis did not seem at all the kind of person who would have written The Chronicles of Narnia, but when Douglas noticed a large wardrobe in the hall, and asked – rather hesitantly – whether it was *the* wardrobe, Jack smiled and said "It might be ..."

Jack got on well with Douglas and David, and he dedicated his new book, *The Horse and his Boy,* to them. As time went by, Jack grew to like Joy more and more. But when, at last, they fell in love and decided to get married it did not look as if they would have very much happiness together. Joy had been taken into hospital where it was found that she had cancer.

Jack with David and Douglas and Susie the dog

Joy was not expected to live and as Jack waited for his wife to die, his sad memories of his mother's death from the same disease kept coming back to him.

Miraculously, Joy got better and she and Jack had some very happy years together. They visited Ireland and they took a trip to Greece with Jack's old friend Roger Lancelyn Green and his wife. Then, sadly, the cancer returned.

Writing to one of his young friends, Jack said: "My wife is very, very ill. I am sure Aslan knows best and whether He leaves her with me or takes her to His own country, He will do what is right ..." Joy eventually died in 1960.

Jack was deeply upset and in one of his last books he described his feelings about losing Joy and how, for a while, he had come to doubt the goodness of the God he had written so much about.

For young Douglas and David and for Warnie it took a long time to get over Joy's death. Jack never quite managed it, although his Christian faith ended up stronger than it was before.

After several months of illness, Jack himself died on 22 November 1963. Although he was such a famous man, the news of his death was over-shadowed by the assassination, on the same day in America, of President John F. Kennedy.

A scene from a television production of the first Chronicle of Narnia

A programme from one of the many stage versions of Jack's books

At the time of his death, Jack was planning to make some final corrections to his stories for a new edition of The Chronicles of Narnia. But, before he could do so, he was, like his characters at the end of *The Last Battle* "beginning Chapter One of the Great Story which no one on earth has read: which goes on forever; in which every chapter is better than the one before".

Since they first began to appear, The Chronicles of Narnia have become some of the most popular books ever written for children.

As well as Jack's own books, dozens of other books have been written about him and what he wrote. There are C. S. Lewis societies in Britain and America and several special magazines are published containing articles and essays about him and his friends.

The Chronicles themselves have been illustrated by a number of artists, although none of them have captured the Land of Narnia in quite the same magical way as the books' original illustrator, Pauline Baynes.

There have been guides and companions to the Narnia books, and the characters have even appeared on calendars and in fantasy role-playing books.

The White Witch comes to life on stage in a production of "The Lion, the Witch and the Wardrobe"

The stories have been dramatised as stage plays and serials for radio and television: one of them was made into a cartoon film and all of them have been read on records and tapes by famous actors and actresses.

Today, the books have a greater number of readers than ever before. It is hard to say exactly why The Chronicles of Narnia remain so popular, except that C. S. Lewis put so many good things into the stories that whether you enjoy them as thrilling adventures or for the "hidden story" behind them, they seem to appeal to everyone.

Actor Joss Ackland as C. S. Lewis in the film about his life, "Shadowlands"

When C. S. Lewis was alive, young readers often used to write and ask him why he did not write some more books about Aslan's world. "I'm afraid I've said all I have to say about Narnia," he wrote to one boy, "but why don't you try to write one yourself? I was writing stories before I was your age, and if you try, I'm sure you will find it great fun." There are, as C. S. Lewis said in a letter to a young girl, several gaps in Narnian history. "I've left you plenty of hints," he wrote, "especially where Lucy and the unicorn are talking in *The Last Battle*."

Perhaps, even though it can't be published, *you* will write a new story about Narnia for your own pleasure but even if you don't you can still enjoy reading C. S. Lewis's books again and again, because the story they tell is one which goes on forever ...